Mental Health
CASE MANAGEMENT

*To my wife, as well as all of the case managers
who are a constant inspiration for this work.*

—Shaun M. Eack, PhD

To case managers, with thanks for their work.

—Catherine G. Greeno, PhD

Mental Health
CASE MANAGEMENT

A Practical Guide

Shaun M. Eack

Carol M. Anderson

Catherine G. Greeno

University of Pittsburgh

Los Angeles | London | New Delhi
Singapore | Washington DC

Los Angeles | London | New Delhi
Singapore | Washington DC

FOR INFORMATION:

SAGE Publications, Inc.
2455 Teller Road
Thousand Oaks, California 91320
E-mail: order@sagepub.com

SAGE Publications Ltd.
1 Oliver's Yard
55 City Road
London EC1Y 1SP
United Kingdom

SAGE Publications India Pvt. Ltd.
B 1/I 1 Mohan Cooperative Industrial Area
Mathura Road, New Delhi 110 044
India

SAGE Publications Asia-Pacific Pte. Ltd.
3 Church Street
#10-04 Samsung Hub
Singapore 049483

Printed in the United States of America.

Library of Congress Cataloging-in-Publication Data

Eack, Shaun M.

Mental health case management : a practical guide / Shaun M. Eack, Carol M. Anderson, Catherine G. Greeno.

p. cm.
Includes bibliographical references and index.

ISBN 978-1-4522-3526-4 (pbk.)

1. Mentally ill--Care. 2. Mental health services. 3. Management. I. Anderson, Carol M., 1939- II. Greeno, Catherine G. III. Title.

RC480.53.E23 2013
3623.19689—dc23   2012010924

This book is printed on acid-free paper.

Acquisitions Editor: Kassie Graves
Editorial Assistant: Elizabeth Luizzi
Production Editor: Laureen Gleason
Copy Editor: Megan Granger
Typesetter: C&M Digitals (P) Ltd.
Proofreader: Cheryl Rivard
Indexer: Karen Wiley
Cover Designer: Candice Harman
Marketing Manager: Lisa Brown
Permissions Editor: Adele Hutchinson

SUSTAINABLE FORESTRY INITIATIVE
Certified Chain of Custody
Promoting Sustainable Forestry
www.sfiprogram.org
SFI-01268

SFI label applies to text stock

12 13 14 15 16 10 9 8 7 6 5 4 3 2 1

Brief Contents

Detailed Contents

Remembering and Respecting the Dignity of the Individual

You are about to take on an important and challenging job helping some of the most vulnerable individuals in society use their strengths to recover from serious mental disorders. Many will have lost their independence, initiative, and creativity from years of repeated episodes of illness and ineffective treatment in institutions. It is crucial to remember that despite their psychiatric disabilities, they also will have strengths, goals, and the need for recognition—just as the rest of us do. They deserve a chance to pursue their forgotten dreams and to use their abilities to establish independent and fulfilling lives. They are experts in what they will need to progress in their journeys toward more functional and rewarding lives. With your help, and using the principles of recovery, they can take advantage of opportunities that have been beyond their grasp. With your help, they can move from the edges of society's tolerance to become full and productive members of their communities. Without your help, and without help from the rest of the team assigned to their care, they risk remaining on the margins, trapped in a cycle of repeated hospitalizations and failure.

As a case manager, you can play a crucial role in helping these individuals cope with their illness by using their own strengths to make the transition to a new life. It all begins with your establishing a collaborative relationship that respects their dignity and strengths. Based on this respect, you will work with these individuals, empowering them to accomplish *their* goals. This manual is designed to give you a brief introduction to the common issues you will encounter during your work and some of the basic knowledge you will need to address these issues. It does not represent a prescription for what to do *to* people but, rather, what you can do *with* people to help them lead the most fulfilling lives possible. Good case managers know that respecting the dignity of those they serve always comes first. Whether you are working to help individuals access services during an acute crisis or to accomplish a positive goal such as living independently or finding a job, you will need to find ways to preserve their self-respect and foster their autonomy. With this focus as a foundation, you will be able to develop a collaborative and empowering relationship that provides opportunities to facilitate real progress and change. You will become increasingly aware of the profound (but too-often overlooked) capabilities of persons with severe mental illness. As you help them use these capabilities and accumulate small successes, you will also become aware that your job as a case manager is, above all, honorable and important work.

Acknowledgments

The authors would like to acknowledge Stephen Christian-Michaels for his feedback and critical support in developing this book. This work was supported in part by National Institute of Mental Health grant MH-66872 to Dr. Anderson.

SAGE and the authors gratefully acknowledge the contributions of the following reviewers: Rebekah F. Cole, Old Dominion University; Julia M. Forman, Walden University; LaKeisha L. Harris, University of Maryland Eastern Shore; Bonnie F. Hatchett, University of Arkansas–Pine Bluff; Brandon Hunt, Pennsylvania State University; Michael A. Mancini, Saint Louis University; and Rebecca G. McBride, Old Dominion University.

1

Introduction

❖ IMPORTANCE OF THE CASE MANAGER IN COMMUNITY MENTAL HEALTH

A good case manager is probably the most important professional in the lives of severely mentally ill individuals recovering in the community. Psychiatrists may prescribe medicine, therapists may provide therapy, and employment specialists may help find jobs, but good case managers make the work of all these professionals possible. They help connect people with services, coordinate care, and ensure that what is being provided is relevant to the current needs and dreams of specific individuals. Whether these individuals have experienced months, or even years, of confusion from unremitting delusions or voices, repeated mood swings, social isolation, or the difficulties in adjusting to life in the community after decades in a psychiatric hospital, all will benefit from case management done right. In fact, in a time of limited and fragmented community resources, many individuals would receive little help at all if not for the abilities of case managers reaching out to engage and connect people to the range of services they need. Case managers worth their salt are lifesavers, because services are of little use to people who cannot access them!

1

The value of community resources and the mental health system is dependent on case managers who are able to form trusting relationships with the individuals assigned to their care, who are available when needed, and who facilitate access to all the formal and informal resources needed by those struggling with mental illnesses. We believe it is crucial for the few very special people tasked with this job to receive the support and information needed to make a *real* difference. In recognition of your vital role as case managers, this manual has been created to ensure you have the basic practical information and ongoing support for the important work you do.

❖ WHY A MANUAL FOR CASE MANAGEMENT?

There are those who think case management simply requires good intentions and a good heart, that it is limited to completing unskilled tasks that facilitate the "real" work done by psychiatrists and therapists. Nothing could be further from the truth. The central role you will perform as a case manager in today's community mental health system requires that you not only be prepared to address the emotional and practical needs of individuals who once were the focus of a range of professionals and institutions but that you address them even more comprehensively. The tasks involved require a breadth of knowledge that parallels a triple doctorate, as well as the negotiating skills and community connections of the slickest politician.

Unfortunately, because case management sometimes appears simple to those who are unaware of the long-term ramifications of serious mental illnesses (and, unfortunately, these are sometimes those who control the purse strings), many case managers are not provided adequate training or adequate support for their work. In fact, if new case managers don't happen to come with experience in mental health (and many do not), they are often thrown into the fray without any idea of how to manage the symptoms and needs of those with mental illness or how to address the challenges of maintaining a recovery focus, much less the specifics of how to help individuals apply for Social Security or how to write a useful progress note. Although some public systems have case managers with advanced degrees or provide extensive training and supervision, both public and private systems more often approach case management services as though the tasks of the job required only goodwill and common sense. However, any seasoned case manager will tell you that what they do involves a lot more than common sense and that it takes a substantial amount of time and training to become a competent case manager—and even more time and training to become a really good one.

Surprisingly, few efforts have been directed toward providing practical hands-on training that case managers would actually find useful in helping individuals with mental illness and their families. This manual represents an attempt to provide such information. It is designed to be of pragmatic help to new case managers while they are being mentored to do their jobs with recovering individuals with mental illness living in the community. The contents of this manual were drafted by expert case managers and case management mentors, with consultation from scholars in the field of mental health. It is a combination of hard-won "real-world" information and basic state-of-the-art academic knowledge about mental illness, recovery, and case management. The focus is on practical "how-to" information about the work.

❖ HOW TO USE THIS MANUAL

Scope of the Manual

Perhaps the best advice regarding how to use this manual comes from a discussion of what this manual is and is not. To begin, this manual is not a comprehensive presentation of all the skills a case manager needs. Ideally, education, learning, and support should never end, and certainly not with this manual. This work is merely an attempt to provide a brief, accurate, and systematic introduction to the basics of case management practice, which, admittedly, are not all that basic. We apologize up front that the concepts presented here have been at times gravely oversimplified to convey a lot of information briefly so that it will be accessible to time-pressed readers. Because the skills and concepts required by case managers are extensive, trying to absorb this information all at once would exceed the attention span of even the most voracious reader.

As we go along, we will attempt to direct those who want more information about a specific topic to the places where it can be found. This manual covers a lot of ground but is not a replacement for good supervision. It should be used in conjunction with whatever traditional case management supervision and hands-on peer mentoring is available. Both supervision and mentoring are essential in effectively applying what is covered in this text, not to mention in learning the many additional skills that will move you beyond the basic information covered here. Supervision and mentoring will also help you maintain your morale and combat the isolation that can be a part of outreach community work. This text provides guidelines, not hard-and-fast rules. It is up to you and your mentor to adapt these general guidelines to make them relevant to the individuals and situations you encounter.

For Case Managers

If you are a beginning case manager, you can use a review of this manual to orient yourself to the populations you will be seeing and the job you will be doing. Over time, you can use it more like a reference book, a resource where you might find more detailed information and specific suggestions on a variety of topics as you encounter them. You are strongly encouraged to discuss with your mentor or supervisor any questions you have about the content you read. While we have tried to provide basic and clear information, some ideas might be confusing or difficult to apply to the specific individuals you see. If you do not receive regular supervision or mentoring, you should have peers or other agency colleagues with whom you can discuss these guidelines to further develop your own case management skills.

For Supervisors/Mentors

This manual is written so that it can be understood by new and inexperienced case managers, regardless of whether they have a mentor. Some beginners will come with knowledge and experience about mental illness, but in our experience many will be starting from scratch. As a supervisor, or if a mentor is available, this text can serve as a guide for what content should be covered with new employees. For this reason, this manual should be used as a guide, rather than read from cover to cover. An index is provided that will make it possible to match the issues case managers encounter with information that will help them intervene effectively. As a supervisor or mentor, you can point your case managers to chapters providing specific information, allowing you to use your supervisory time more effectively to help them integrate and apply the concepts presented to "real-world" situations. For example, when new case managers do not understand the behaviors of clients, you can suggest that it may help them to review the chapter on the symptoms of severe mental illness. Then you can provide them with the opportunity to discuss with you how these symptoms are influencing client behaviors, how they can understand these symptoms in a way that will increase their ability to help clients reach their goals, or how they can help their clients better manage their symptoms. To be of most help to new case managers, who often have little time to read—and some of whom learn more effectively through face-to face supervision—becoming familiar with the contents of the manual will allow you to direct mentees to specific sections that might be helpful in deciding how to intervene at specific times. Being able to see how general concepts and ideas are encountered in practice will help them integrate the information provided in this manual in their daily work.

2

Getting Started as a Case Manager

The hardest times in *your* life as a case manager are the initial days on the job, especially if you are starting without experience working with individuals with mental illness and without clear instructions about how to help your new clients. Under these circumstances, it would not be surprising if you were initially uncomfortable with your clients, who might behave strangely or wonder what you could possibly do to help them. You might also question exactly what your responsibilities are and how you are supposed to fulfill them. Even if you have experience working in other settings with individuals who have a mental illness, you might be initially uncomfortable working with them in an unstructured environment without the comfort of an office or the immediate availability of supportive colleagues. Fortunately, there are some clear rules of thumb for getting through your first days on the job.

❖ LOGISTICS AND RESPONSIBILITIES

The logistics of being a case manager are pretty straightforward and highlight both the unique and challenging experiences of providing case management services. A good review of these logistics ahead of time will help you know what is expected of you. For instance, it is important to be prepared for the fact that you will not spend much time in an office. The best case managers spend most of their time in the community, connecting with their clients and identifying the services their clients need. You will see clients where they live. You will have sessions in the client's home, in your car en route to the client's doctor's office, or even in a local fast-food restaurant. You will be doing work that is anything but routine, requiring that you maintain an incredibly flexible schedule. You have to be prepared to deal with whatever comes up in the life of a consumer. Your appointments with clients will not be the standard 50-minute hour seen in office-based therapy sessions. Some clients may respond best to 15 minutes of your time, but they may need 15 minutes every day. Others may need you to sometimes spend half a day helping them with one task or another. There will be times when you cannot find a client when you had planned to see him, or times when you have to postpone a planned meeting with one client when another client has an emergency or needs that are suddenly more pressing.

It is crucial to remember that your job as a case manager is not 9 to 5. To facilitate a client's participation in social activities, or in times of crises, you may have to be available to a client well after 5 p.m. or on the weekend. There is rarely a dull moment in case management. It will be hectic at times and slow at other times. This can be exciting but difficult if you have been used to a regular schedule in an agency or institution. If you have difficulty going with the flow or if you require a fixed schedule, this may not be the work for you.

Paperwork

Another important and essential task of case management (and all mental health services) is paperwork. Almost everyone hates paperwork, but keeping up on paperwork is crucial for several reasons. Other professionals are involved with the clients you see, and keeping a paper record of your work with clients helps others know what is going on, when a client is doing well, and when a crisis is brewing. This information can influence their work with your client. In addition, change is often slow in working with individuals with mental illness. The slow nature of change can cause you to lose focus and lose track of the collaborative goals you and your client have set. Paperwork is a useful way to keep your finger on the pulse of the situation, helping you, your client, and the team see that small changes have occurred, contributing to everyone's morale.

Paperwork can seem like an irrelevant and hard-to-manage burden when you are busy and your priority is helping people survive and thrive in their communities, especially when you don't sit at a desk but virtually live in your car. A final fact that should motivate you to do your paperwork in a timely fashion is that your agency needs to document your work for regulatory bodies and in order to be reimbursed for your services. Someone (usually the federal or state government) pays for these services, which in turn pays the rent and *your* salary. No matter how much you work to avoid paperwork, you will only make your supervisors cranky if you don't stay on top of it—and you will end up having to do it in the long run anyway.

Staying up to date on paperwork while continuing to provide effective services requires that you learn good time management. Time management helps you avoid getting overwhelmed and finding yourself on the agency's list of problem employees. A balance can almost always be found between time spent going out and seeing clients and time spent staying in and doing paperwork. Sometimes you can even do double duty by finding a way to complete some of your paperwork between appointments, on the road or as you wait for a client. Conquering paperwork will be critical to your success at any agency, as almost all agencies measure your success, at least in part, by how many people you see and how much time you spend with them. They have no way of knowing how much you are doing to help your clients without you telling them by documenting it.

Basic Responsibilities

Your duties will not be as vast as they might seem. The good news is that you are not responsible for everything. You will certainly have many crucial tasks, but you are not alone in the process of facilitating the recovery of a person with severe mental illness, nor are you responsible for making sure that everything is done this week, month, or even year. You are part of a team, and everyone shares the essential responsibilities of helping those with severe mental illness stay out of the hospital, get what they need to survive in the community, and live the fullest and most satisfying lives possible. These are certainly no small tasks, but you all will have a lot of time to work on them since things move slowly most of the time. To accomplish your essential part of the mission, you start by ensuring that the individuals you see have their basic needs for shelter/food met and basic supports in place so they can focus their energies on recovery. To accomplish this, you need to perform five primary tasks:

- *Develop a good relationship with your clients.* This includes fostering trust and open communication, making it clear to your client that you are there to help. As mentioned earlier, this involves being nonjudgmental, respectful, and compassionate.

- *Broker resources.* It's your job to provide linkage to necessary goods (e.g., housing, food stamps, transportation) and services (e.g., doctors, dentists, therapists). To be helpful, you need to learn about what is available in your particular community. Many agencies have a resource manual, but if not, you can learn from other case managers and then accumulate the things you learn in a binder that the whole staff can use.

- *Assess mental health functioning.* Being vigilant and regularly taking an inventory of your client's mental health status can help prevent acute episodes before they occur and avoid the need for more restrictive care (e.g., keep your eyes open to see if clients are taking their medicine, experiencing more symptoms than usual, drinking or using drugs).

- *Assess life stresses and strains.* Everyone experiences stresses and strains from time to time, but these stresses can exacerbate the symptoms of mental illness or provoke more serious problems. If you keep an eye on what is stressful to your clients in their living arrangements or job placements, you can help them problem-solve to minimize the impact of negative life events.

- *Facilitate recovery.* Ensure that clients are empowered to do what they can on their own (e.g., take the bus to see the doctor, seek out employment opportunities) and that they have the hope and opportunity to achieve their life goals (e.g., go back to school, get a romantic partner, have a respected place in the community). Concentrating on one step at a time is crucial for successfully achieving all these recovery goals. Even the best ideas can be overwhelming if the goal is too ambitious or the pace too fast.

The Need for Continuous Flexibility

The activities listed above form the case manager's primary responsibilities. There will be times when your help is needed more in one area than another. There are times when a client will need more time from you, but there are also times when frequent contact can become a stress. It's great if you can discuss these fluctuations openly with your clients so they can tell you what and how much they need from you.

While "whatever it takes" is a good motto for case management, at times case managers feel pressured to do much more than they should for their clients, unwittingly encouraging dependency. Be careful not to overfunction. A good case manager learns to help clients help themselves rather than doing everything for them. Becoming involved in too many caretaking tasks will ultimately prevent you from effectively accomplishing your primary mission with your clients—moving them toward recovery. It may take much longer to help a client learn to use public transportation to get to doctors' appointments, but this skill will be more useful to the client in the long run than you providing him or her with a ride.

You should be responsible for tasks outside your primary responsibilities only when other ways of achieving these tasks are not available to your client. If your client is lonely, it is better to help him or her connect with a formal or informal network of support rather than stepping into the role of "buddy." As a case manager, providing social contact, transportation, or even therapy should **NOT** be seen as an end in itself. You do these things as a first step in teaching clients to do them for themselves or in showing them how they can get these things from others (e.g., connect them with a peer mentor or drop-in center, help them obtain bus tokens and teach them the bus route, identify the barriers involved in going to therapy sessions, etc.). Remember, if you do more than you are responsible for, who is going to do what you are supposed to do? No one else can or will do what a good case manager does, and that is why it is so important to remember to stay within your primary responsibilities.

This is not to say that as a case manager you should allow the needs of clients to be neglected for the sole purpose of drawing a boundary that marks your primary defined responsibilities. Sometimes appropriate and needed resources are not available, and if you don't step into the breach, no one will. For example, there may not be public transportation for clients who live in rural areas. When they need to get to services or resources, your choice may be between taking them yourself or the clients not getting the help they need. In such cases you will need to adjust your responsibilities to match the limitations of what is available in the community or what the client can manage, while being mindful to move toward helping clients do as much as possible on their own.

Often you will have to show clients how to use new resources. For example, even when there is good public transportation, you may need to ride the bus a few times with a client to show him or her how it works, when and where to catch it, and just generally help the client overcome anxiety about a new experience. How much you should do for your clients is always an open and negotiable question, one that requires you to consider both your basic responsibilities to the work context and the client's needs. What you should and should not do is not governed by hard-and-fast rules but, rather, by what is most important for each client in each situation.

How You Do Things Is Just as Important as What You Do

As you can see from all the responsibilities that rest on your shoulders as a case manager, there will be many different tasks you will perform and opportunities you will seize in helping your clients recover. It is important to remember that while you will be very busy with "things to do," case management is not an impersonal task of brokering resources, monitoring psychiatric status, and supporting independence. You are working with people. People have their own ideas, hopes, and dreams. They want to take ownership of their lives and independently do things that maximize their strengths. You can be doing all the right things as a case manager and taking responsibility for all the tasks listed above, but if you do not take the time to build a relationship and listen to your client, your activities will be sterile. Clients who feel as though you have not listened to them and understood their perspective will feel they are victims of cookie-cutter case management, making them skeptical of your skills and resistant to engagement, no matter the potential helpfulness of the resources you are bringing them.

In addition, while case managers have a lot of concrete responsibilities, you are more than a technician. A good case manager not only provides a stable environment but also serves as a confidant, a spring of hope, and an inspiration. You will need to work daily not only to help your clients get the resources they need but also to paint a positive and realistic picture for the future. You will need to help individuals dream about a life beyond their psychiatric condition and to empower them to seize opportunities that will elevate their self-esteem and place in the world. As a case manager, it is sometimes easy to forget that you may be the person on the team who spends the most time with clients, the one who is most aware of the details and challenges in their daily lives. You may be the person they are most likely to turn to for advice in times of crisis or when they are simply in need of realistic hope for the future. The responsibility to look beyond the technical aspects of your work and facilitate the recovery of the whole person is one of the things that elevates the practice of case management to the status of a profession. As you go through this manual and your daily activities, you should always remember this higher calling.

❖ YOUR FIRST CLIENTS

Now that you know what to expect from the job and what the job expects from you, you are likely on your way to seeing your first clients. Okay now, *B-R-E-A-T-H-E*. Remember that everyone has some insecurity about how effective they will be in any new job, even if they have been well trained. If you do not have a mentor or peer who has offered to take you along on some visits to his or her clients, try to find someone who will do this so you won't be completely green. You can't prevent things from being rocky at first. In fact, it is perfectly fine if your first sessions with clients resemble a crash course with a lot of trial-and-error learning. You will make mistakes. Don't be afraid to admit them and apologize. When things don't go well, they are best taken as learning experiences so that next time things go better.

One of the most important things you can do just before you see each of your clients (in addition to remaining calm) is to be as prepared as possible. This includes

- reading up on your client's mental health and diagnostic assessment information, focusing on what the person's strengths might be and what problems he or she may be experiencing;

- brainstorming ideas for how to help this client with your mentor, supervisor, or other case managers who have worked with this client or clients with similar problems; and

- trying to define the purpose of each of your contacts with the client and the tasks that should be accomplished.

Having this information will provide you with a structure that will allow you to make the most of your time with the client, help you concentrate on establishing a good relationship, and help those first meetings go smoothly.

During your visits with clients, it is important to do all that you can to convey respect and a genuine willingness to be helpful. This includes beginning with the basic social graces, such as shaking hands and smiling as you greet the client, just as you would when greeting anyone else for the first time. It also helps to start with a bit of social conversation about totally nonthreatening topics, based on what the client seems interested in. What he is wearing and what is in his environment might provide clues. For instance, does he have a cap from a local sports team, a dog or cat, particular posters on the walls? Commenting on these can get a conversation started and begin to put your client at ease. In this brief introductory interaction, the importance of communicating warmth and caring cannot be overstated, although it must be genuine and not overdone. Many clients will be nervous about seeing you, and some will be distrustful about seeing a stranger at all. If the first contact seems overly tense, it is perfectly reasonable to cut it short and assure the client that you will be back. If you are kind but not intrusive, if you express interest in them and their lives, you will eventually break the ice.

It is also important that you take the time to listen to the client and his description of how things are going. To keep focused, it's good to come into every session with a specific but limited goal, even if this is just to reinforce your connection with a client. People usually want to feel understood and welcome a chance to tell their stories once they are comfortable. However, it's important to let the client set the agenda and the pace for sharing. That means listening to what the client says he needs and letting him know you are listening by repeating back what you think you have heard or by asking questions. Only when you think you clearly understand what the client wants should you move to look at ways of addressing whatever problem or issue he has noted. For example, after clients tell you they have no money, you might ask a few questions about how they got into this state before moving to say something like, "Well, we better figure out how you can get your bills paid this month."

Responding to client-expressed needs in the moment requires you to have the flexibility to change your agenda and plans for the session. Even if you believe a topic you planned to address is crucial, try first to follow the client's agenda, and then raise your own. For the many things you cannot change for the client, it is important to convey some level of empathy and understanding of the hardship of the situation. For example, after a client tells you about a bad fight he had with his girlfriend, you should empathize with him and provide support without assuming you know how he feels. You might say, "How was that for you? Was it really difficult?" or "Relationships are tough for everybody when they don't go well, but it's great that you have been able to hang in there with her." It's not your job to try to fix the relationship, but you can be there to support your client and show him that you are trying to understand what he is going through. This tends to be one of the best methods of building a good helping relationship.

Use Your Supervisors and Mentors

In most agencies you will have an administrative supervisor whom you will tend to see in the office. If you have a mentor who is more of a peer, that person will have a practice of his or her own and should be showing you the ropes out in the field and providing you with the practical, day-to-day information you need to be an effective case manager. When you first start, most agencies will have you shadow your mentor or a peer for a couple of weeks so that he or she can show you the ropes. Then you will probably be given a small caseload. In your early contacts with clients, your mentor will probably periodically accompany you and give you pointers about what you could do to be more helpful. After you get started, you can use your mentor more as a resource for getting answers to specific questions, clarifying anything you are confused about, or just sharing your anxiety to get some peer support.

Since the first days (or, actually, months) of being a case manager include a lot of learning, tons of new information, and perhaps some anxiety, it is important to get in the habit of using the expertise of supervisors and, if available, mentors. What gets in the way of learning for most beginners is not effectively using supervisors and mentors because they fear looking bad or incompetent. Rather than hiding what you see as your mistakes, try to be honest. Share your concerns and even your horror stories. Supervisors and mentors are there to help you learn to put basic principles into practice with specific clients, as well as to help you with the specific aspects of the agency that cannot be covered here or in any written description of the job. They feel good if they can be helpful to you. Ask questions. No one expects you to know everything, so now is the time to get information rather than worry about impressing them. Your mentor and/or supervisor can help you understand your clients, set priorities, and define appropriate tasks so you can begin taking care of whatever needs to be done before you next see your client. They may even have gone through this manual and are ready to help you apply the concepts you are learning to your practice in the real world.

Maintain a Focus on Tasks

Each session should end having produced a task that you want to complete before you see the client next, and in your early days as a case manager you may not know exactly what task is needed or how to complete it. If you find that your sessions with clients tend to end without defining any specific task for either you or your client to accomplish before the next session, you are probably not making the most out of your meetings and should work with your client, mentor, and supervisor to figure out what specific tasks would contribute to your client's achievement of one of his or her goals. Of course, very few meetings with a client will be about completing large tasks, such as moving to an independent residence or getting a job. These large overall goals are important, but, from contact to contact, you will usually be taking only small steps toward getting them accomplished. A step toward obtaining a job may involve improved hygiene, getting up at a regular hour, or getting comfortable with a social conversation. Improvement in severe mental illness is usually incredibly slow, which can be frustrating for the client and the case manager alike. Because of this, you may not always have new tasks to work on with clients. Rather, your meetings may be about reinforcing trust in the relationship, monitoring changes in client status, or working to revise or complete an existing task that may be taking longer than expected.

When setting goals and tasks with clients, it is always important to remember to start slowly and break goals into small steps. Working with a client on small tasks or taking a while to get a task done should not be a concern as long as you are consistently working toward the client's goal. In fact, small tasks are the most useful because accomplishing them creates small successes that can build your client's confidence. Most beginning case managers try to accomplish too much and assign tasks that are too ambitious. If you fall into this trap and the client is unable to do the task, you should overtly take responsibility for the error of assigning too much, rather than leaving the client demoralized and feeling like a failure. Admit you have made a misstep, and assign something easier.

❖ WORKING WITH OTHER PROFESSIONALS

As a case manager, you must coordinate services provided by many different disciplines in many different settings. This requires that you work as a team (even if a team isn't defined) with a variety of people, both in the mental health field and beyond. Whenever you work with other professionals from other agencies, you are always representing not only your client but also your department, agency, and the profession of case management in general. Therefore, it is important that you act professionally and cooperatively, or you will not be able to do what you need to do to help your clients. When you have meetings with other professionals, dress for the occasion. Dressing casually in jeans and running shoes is fine for many of the tasks you will have to do in case management, but you will be far less likely to be heard or taken seriously if you show up for meetings with psychiatrists or other social service professionals in T-shirts with holes in them. How you look and everything you do with these colleagues will influence how effective you are in helping your clients get what they need.

While the services you connect people to may be quite diverse, mental health and social service agencies are part of a small world. The people in this world will treat you well and give more attention to your clients once you develop a reputation as someone who is a serious professional committed to clients and respectful of the role other people play in helping them. The same advice goes for working with those within your agency. Case managers will frequently be part of a team, such as an Assertive Community Treatment team, of professionals within their agency. When you are working as part of a team, every action you take with clients has the potential to affect the work of other members of the team. It is important to facilitate the effectiveness of this team by staying in touch with other team members and actively participating in team meetings on behalf of your clients so that services can be effectively coordinated. If important things happen with your client, you should relay this information to your fellow team members as soon as possible. This will allow them to provide you with help when needed or modify their own treatment and goals if necessary. As the client's case manager, you should try always to be at the table when decisions about the client's treatment plans are made. It is entirely possible that you will know some of the team's clients better than other professionals who see them less frequently, but it does not help anyone to tell them so. Good case managers avoid power struggles or acting as though they are the only ones with a valid opinion. You will earn the respect and trust of the team by listening thoughtfully to the other team members' ideas and contributing information only when appropriate.

❖ WORKING WITH FAMILIES

Most of the clients you see will have chosen to live or been placed in group homes, residential care, or independent apartments. Nonetheless, some may live with their families, and even when they do not, a high percentage of clients will be in frequent contact with various family members. There will certainly be times when family members do not want to be involved in the recovery process, and times when clients would rather not have their families involved. But both clients and their families will often welcome the chance to reconnect. These are important ties that should be encouraged because they offer a level of commitment no other social contact can. If your client is a young adult, you may be too eager to help him or her be independent, seeing family contact as a deterrent to the client's emancipation. However, if family members have continued to be involved with a client despite a long-term illness, they are likely to constitute an important resource that could support client strengths and facilitate recovery.

Family members, in fact, can be one of the best resources for learning how to serve a client. Their awareness of the client's history can allow them to share information that may not have been documented in old charts. Their long-term relationship with your client also puts them in a position of being able to tell you and the team what interventions have worked in the past, affording you insights about what to do when progress seems to have stalled or at least allowing you to think carefully before barging ahead with a plan that has failed before. They can help you identify early warning signs that indicate that their loved one may be getting sick again, having witnessed patterns of idiosyncratic behaviors that seem to have preceded psychotic episodes in the past (e.g., sleeping less, reading the Bible more, becoming paranoid or depressed). Finally, family members can be some of the best natural supports for clients and their recovery. It is often advantageous for the case manager to partner with family members in order to provide the best care to clients with serious mental illness. Families may be able to help out with tasks aimed at recovery or to provide encouragement and reinforce client motivation. Consequently, case managers should never ignore this important resource and should enlist the help of family members whenever they can. If the client and family have become alienated over the years, getting consent from the client to develop these important ties gradually is in order. And be sure to remember that when engaging families, you will need the client's permission (often in written form) to discuss the client with the family. Also remember that if you involve families, keep them in the loop. You will be busy as a case manager, but don't let this fall by the wayside. Families can help only if they are informed about *what is going on*. With your client's permission, you should stay in regular contact with the family to keep them up to date about where things stand and to give them an opportunity to provide you with feedback about their views.

❖ WORKING WITH ISSUES OF CULTURE, RACE, AND CLASS

Cultural values and norms shape much of how everyone views the world, mental illness, and the professionals involved in facilitating recovery from a psychiatric disability. You will see clients with mental illness whose characteristics, backgrounds, and life experiences differ from your own. They will come from other classes, races, ethnicities, religious affiliations, and geographical locations. Their unique backgrounds will have shaped their worldviews, ways of coping, and how they will respond to your efforts to help them. Background and culture will predict clients' tolerance of their mental illness, how they express their symptoms, the importance they place on self-reliance, their willingness to accept various types of help, and the amount of shame and stigma they associate with their illness. For instance, Latinos tend to view mental illness as a physical ailment, and, indeed, distressed individuals from these cultures often present with symptoms more physical in nature and would clearly prefer help from a primary care physician rather than a mental health professional. African Americans, especially those living in poverty, also tend to avoid seeking formal psychiatric services, instead preferring to rely on family and pastoral support to cope with mental health problems. In fact, this tendency is widely believed to account for the statistics showing less use of and compliance with mental health services by African Americans, especially young African American males. The potential use of psychiatric services by those from many Asian cultures is probably influenced by views that mental illness is associated with spiritual conflict, or views of such shame that mental illness can prevent even the siblings of the ill person from getting married.

Dealing with the diversity of views about mental illness and its treatment requires that you become sensitive to how cultural variables impact values, attitudes, behaviors, and receptivity to help. You will unwittingly communicate a lack of understanding and respect for who clients are and what they believe, generating challenges and resistance. It would be relatively easy to recommend sensitivity to the possibility that Latino clients will see mental illnesses through the lens of physical symptoms, African American clients will be influenced by values of family privacy and the importance of religion, and Asian clients by shame and views of the spiritual causes, but the influence of these factors is oversimplified even within a given culture, not to mention that many cultures are not even addressed in this description. In addition, you will bring your own culture and its own unique views of mental illness and coping to the relationship. It will be far too easy to become judgmental about the behaviors of people who are different from you. Clearly, it is impossible for us to suggest ways for you to deal with clients from all the multiple cultures you will encounter. The specific issues are many and complex, and beyond the scope of this manual. We choose instead to suggest the importance of bridging difference by asking clients about their views, their values, and the meanings of their behaviors. Be prepared to ask questions about these issues, listen to their answers, and then tailor what you offer to match the way your clients see their illness and their problems. It is important to also ask how your clients feel about working with someone from another ethnic or racial group. Knowing if there is a potential problem is the first step to bridging the gap. Use what you learn to determine the need for support for clients who experience discrimination or stigma, how you should deliver information about the illness, and which resources are potentially appropriate sources of help. This brief assessment will help you discuss mental illness and coping in ways that you think your clients will be able to hear and accept and allow you to connect them with resources they are particularly likely to perceive as beneficial. For instance, when clients report strong family bonds, you might choose to solicit their family's help in engaging them.

Finally, it is important to remember that despite the considerable progress of advocacy groups, such as the National Alliance on Mental Illness, considerable stigma about mental illness remains. The predominant view of mental illness in the United States is a medical view that locates the source of psychiatric conditions in the brain. However, many subcultures do not totally accept the medical model of mental illness, making it exceptionally difficult for individuals and families from some minority groups to accept the presence of a psychiatric disability or mental health treatment. Stigma is often significantly magnified for those minority groups who already experience themselves as being disrespected by the dominant culture. You should be prepared to accept their ambivalence about you and psychiatric services in general, and work to develop trust and connection. Their resistance is not a personal affront to your abilities but a legitimate concern about the impact of the additional stigma that can result from becoming part of the mental health system.

3

The Recovery Model

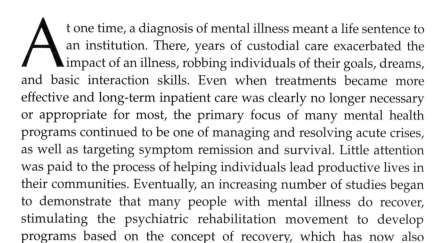

At one time, a diagnosis of mental illness meant a life sentence to an institution. There, years of custodial care exacerbated the impact of an illness, robbing individuals of their goals, dreams, and basic interaction skills. Even when treatments became more effective and long-term inpatient care was clearly no longer necessary or appropriate for most, the primary focus of many mental health programs continued to be one of managing and resolving acute crises, as well as targeting symptom remission and survival. Little attention was paid to the process of helping individuals lead productive lives in their communities. Eventually, an increasing number of studies began to demonstrate that many people with mental illness do recover, stimulating the psychiatric rehabilitation movement to develop programs based on the concept of recovery, which has now also become a cornerstone of effective case management.

The recovery model offers an approach to mental illness that goes beyond a focus on symptoms. It involves an emphasis on the strengths individuals have despite their illness, maximizing their chances of building new, productive, and more fulfilling lives. The recovery model provides a more hopeful response to individuals rather than simply defining them by their illnesses, as if that would explain the totality of their being. Rather, its basic philosophy of respect and self-determination promotes a collaboration between professionals and consumers as they work to regain any skills and abilities they may have lost during their illness, as well as ones they now need in order to achieve their goals and dreams. This chapter will provide an overview of the philosophy and components of the recovery model and discuss how it can help you in your practice as a case manager.

❖ WHAT IS RECOVERY?

Recovery is a concept earlier used in substance abuse, which regarded addiction as a chronic problem but one with which individuals could lead productive lives through a long-term process of self-management. Recovery in the context of mental illness has similarities and differences. It has been defined by consumers, families, and professionals broadly as "a journey of healing and transformation enabling a person with a mental health problem to live a meaningful life in a community of his or her choice while striving to achieve his or her full potential."* An inherent property of this definition is that recovery is a process, with some people achieving their goals in a relatively short time and others working toward recovery throughout their lives. Today, recovery has come to be seen as a legitimate focus for psychiatric systems of care, and one that involves the provision of support and assistance as individuals set goals and engage in the process of getting their lives back after having experienced a mental illness.

Facilitating recovery in case management first involves ensuring the provision of basic necessities and services, such as housing and health care. However, it is also based on developing a respectful and collaborative relationship that encourages hope, self-determination, and a network of supportive contacts. As a case manager, you will facilitate recovery by ensuring that individuals are involved in all the decisions about their care and their lives, consistently demonstrating respect for their priorities and needs. You will provide information as needed about the possible ramifications of their decisions, and provide clients with coping strategies they can use to become experts on managing their condition.

❖ COMPONENTS OF RECOVERY

To help make the concept of recovery even more concrete, 10 distinct and crucial components of recovery have been identified.* They represent

---

*Substance Abuse and Mental Health Services Administration (2004).

the basic philosophy of recovery and should guide your work as a case manager.

- *Recovery is self-directed.* Too often, professionals seem to believe it is their role to make all decisions for those with psychiatric disabilities, whether about their treatment or their lives. They act as if the individual's opinions are irrelevant. It is crucial that you respect your clients' abilities to determine their own fate, even to make their own mistakes. You can provide input, but self-direction means the client should lead and direct the process.

- *Recovery is individualized.* What is crucial to achieving and building a fulfilling life will differ from person to person. For some it will mean reconnecting with family, for others finding meaningful work, and for still others finally having a safe place to call home. It is important to help clients define their own priorities and goals and create their own unique definition of what recovery means.

- *Recovery involves empowerment.* A key component of the process of recovery is working to empower clients by actively helping them participate in the process of their own treatment. Actually, clients have their own power if we professionals do not unintentionally take it away by unilaterally setting their goals or making decisions for them. Making decisions on behalf of clients rather than with them sabotages their developing autonomy. You can better help them develop their strengths by supporting their efforts to take the reins of their lives and determine their own futures.

- *Recovery is holistic.* Central to the definition of recovery is the notion that a fulfilling life is rich and consists of many different aspects. Friends, family, work, education, and the like are but a few of the things most of us would consider key ingredients to a good quality of life. The process of recovery requires that you work with clients to determine their views of what would make their lives meaningful and fulfilling, help them define which one is their current first priority, and then work with them on it in a thoughtful way. Throughout this manual you will see we emphasize taking one step at a time. Whatever the topic, one step at a time helps both you and your client not become overwhelmed.

- *Recovery is nonlinear.* This is a fancy way of saying that recovery does not necessarily follow an ordered step-by-step process. There is no set Recovery Step #1 or predetermined Recovery Step #20. People proceed in their own recovery in ways that ebb and flow with their lives and experiences. Success or failure at one goal will determine the choice of the next step. Sometimes it is a process of two steps forward and one step back. These experiences teach both you and your client about the process and what should come next.

- *Recovery is strengths-based.* While all the clients you see will have challenges and difficulties, they will also all have at least some strengths. Recovery is about identifying and emphasizing these strengths to overcome challenges and build a good quality of life.

- *Recovery requires peer support.* Finding ways to involve clients with others who have psychiatric disabilities provides them with opportunities for support and role models who may be further along in the process of recovery. Peer contacts also decrease the isolation and loneliness often involved in the early stages of recovery.

- *Recovery requires respect.* The job of a case manager is to demonstrate respect for clients in a variety of ways. Recovery involves your listening to clients and asking for their opinions. It also involves helping them when they encounter the challenges of living with the stigma of a psychiatric disability. You should be prepared to help them manage impacts of their disability as well as act in ways that will allow them to become accepted members of the community.

- *Recovery requires clients taking responsibility.* Your client's recovery is not your responsibility as a case manager; you are only a facilitator of the process. Recovery is the responsibility of the client and should remain in the hands of the client. Your role is to provide expertise and consultation along the way.

- *Recovery requires hope.* Perhaps the most important aspect of the process of recovery is helping your clients develop hope for a better future. Clients need to believe that conditions improve and their goals are possible, given time. For years professionals worried about providing "false hope" to their clients, but research has shown us that many individuals with mental illnesses are able to develop productive lives despite the barriers they encounter. Recovery is about dreaming big and helping your clients develop a vision for where they want to go and how they want to get there, one step at a time. None of this is possible without some consistent reassurance from you that there is hope for a better future.

These 10 principles represent the core components of the recovery model of psychiatric rehabilitation that are particularly relevant to you as a case manager. As you can see, they are pretty much a set of common-sense principles that provide a guiding framework for helping those who have serious mental illnesses. In fact, many of these concepts are key tenants of good clinical practice with any population. The idea that clients should take an active role in their own recovery is not unique. Neither is the importance of hope as clients struggle to see beyond their current difficulties. There may be times when both you and your clients become overwhelmed with the challenges of coping with mental illness, and even with the challenges of the bureaucratic barriers we must negotiate on our clients' behalf. Becoming temporarily overwhelmed can cause you both to feel hopeless or to forget the strength-based emphasis of your work together. In this process, your mission is to maintain the client relationship in ways that respect the slow nature of change and the humanity of your encounter with each other.

❖ RECOVERY AND CASE MANAGEMENT

As a case manager, you are in a vital position to facilitate client recovery, particularly as you develop a working knowledge of resources and practical skills for coping with problems. The integration of a recovery philosophy and its principles into your case management can and should occur in many ways. It will be important, overall, to support client independence steadfastly. As noted in Chapter 2, a key case management principle is to refrain from doing for clients what they can do for themselves. Doing things for clients may provide them with some temporary relief, but habitually rescuing them will not help them develop their inherent capabilities and take personal responsibility for their own recovery.

As a case manager, you incorporate the holistic principle of recovery by paying attention to all aspects of clients' lives that are influenced by and in turn impact their mental health. The concept of attending to the whole person, and not just his or her psychiatric disability, provides you with another way of supporting your clients' recovery. As we've just mentioned, you should not do everything for your clients, but you can and should assess their needs for housing, dental care, and financial help. You can and should be ready to assess and facilitate client connections to family members and peers. The principle involved is starting where your client is. If he or she initially needs substantial help, you can provide it, gradually supporting more and more autonomy. This means your practice will need to be individualized and tailored to the unique strengths and needs of the individuals you serve at various points in time.

Finally, perhaps the most important role you will play in the recovery of your clients is facilitating and maintaining hope. If your clients have been ill for an extended period of time, they may have all but lost hope when you first arrive on the scene. You will initially see clients in their worst moments, when they feel as though they have nothing left and have nowhere to turn. You will probably have more contact with your clients than they have with their family or onetime friends. You may become the most important relationship in their lives until you can help them form a support network. In such circumstances, your job will be to help them begin to have some semblance of a good life. To many clients, achieving any goal will seem insurmountable, and, indeed, some will have lost all hope of being successful. You must then be ready to reassure clients that you will work together to overcome the challenges, that a better future is not only possible but likely. You do not need to worry about providing false hope; your biggest concern is providing false despair. The hope that you provide your clients will not only lift their spirits but will empower them to achieve things they had come to believe were impossible.

4

Being an Ethical
Case Manager

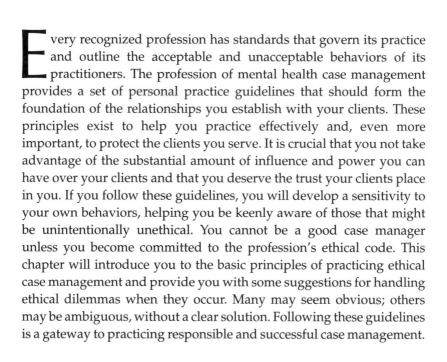

E very recognized profession has standards that govern its practice
and outline the acceptable and unacceptable behaviors of its
practitioners. The profession of mental health case management
provides a set of personal practice guidelines that should form the
foundation of the relationships you establish with your clients. These
principles exist to help you practice effectively and, even more
important, to protect the clients you serve. It is crucial that you not take
advantage of the substantial amount of influence and power you can
have over your clients and that you deserve the trust your clients place
in you. If you follow these guidelines, you will develop a sensitivity to
your own behaviors, helping you be keenly aware of those that might
be unintentionally unethical. You cannot be a good case manager
unless you become committed to the profession's ethical code. This
chapter will introduce you to the basic principles of practicing ethical
case management and provide you with some suggestions for handling
ethical dilemmas when they occur. Many may seem obvious; others
may be ambiguous, without a clear solution. Following these guidelines
is a gateway to practicing responsible and successful case management.

❖ PERSONAL PRACTICE GUIDELINES OF CASE MANAGEMENT

The "personal practice guidelines" listed in Table 4.1 below were established by the National Association of Case Management.[1] They outline behaviors that reflect the standard code of ethics for mental health case managers. These guidelines provide 20 statements that should guide your relationships with clients, regardless of their gender, race, religion, sexual orientation, and level of functioning. Core to each specific point is the need for you to respect the dignity of all your clients. This includes respecting their privacy and fostering healthy relationships with your clients and avoiding harmful ones. *Above all, you must strive to do no harm to those people who rely on your help.*

Table 4.1   Personal Practice Guidelines of Case Management

As a case manager,
1. I am committed to respect the dignity and autonomy of all persons and to behave in a manner that communicates this respect.
2. I am committed to each individual's right to self-determination, and the rights of people to make their own life choices.
3. I am committed to fight stigma wherever I find it, to educate the community, and to promote community integration for the people I serve.
4. I do not allow my words or actions to reflect prejudice or discrimination regarding a person's race, culture, creed, gender, or sexual orientation.
5. I strive both to seek and provide culturally sensitive services for each person and to continually increase my cultural competence.
6. I am committed to helping persons find or acknowledge their strengths and to use these strengths to achieve their goals.
7. I am committed to helping persons achieve maximum self-responsibility and to find and use services that promote increased knowledge, skills, and competencies.
8. I acknowledge the power of self-help and peer support and encourage participation in these activities with those I serve.
9. I am honest with myself, my colleagues, the people I serve, and others involved in their care.

[1]National Association of Case Management (2005).

10. I keep confidential all information entrusted to me by those I serve except when to do so puts the person or others at grave risk. I am obligated to explain the limits of confidentiality to the persons I serve at the beginning of our working together.

11. I am committed to a holistic perspective, seeing each person I serve in the context of their family, friends, other significant people in their lives, their community, and their culture, and working within the context of this natural support system.

12. I must strive to maintain healthy relationships with the people I serve, avoiding confusing or multiple relationships and keeping the relationship focused on the individual's needs, not my own.

13. I maintain a commitment to prevent crisis situations with the people I serve, to present and support crisis alternatives, to develop an advanced instruction crisis plan with the individual whenever possible, and to avoid forced treatment unless there is a clear and present danger to the person served or another.

14. I have an obligation to consult with my supervisor, obtain training, or refer to a more qualified case manager any individual with a need I do not feel capable of addressing.

15. I have an obligation to remain curious—learning, growing, developing, and using opportunities for continuing education in my field or profession.

16. I am committed to a regular assessment of my service recipients' expectations of me and to consistently improving my practice to meet their expectations.

17. I have an obligation to advocate for the people I serve, for their rights, for equal treatment, and for resources to meet their needs.

18. I am obligated to learn the laws and regulations governing my practice and to abide by them, including the duty to warn anyone in danger of physical harm and the duty to report physical, sexual, emotional, and/or verbal abuse to the proper person or agency.

19. I am obligated to work supportively with my colleagues and to keep their confidences.

20. I am obligated to urge any colleague who appears impaired to seek help and, failing this, to discuss my concerns with the appropriate agency authority.

❖ BIG ETHICAL PITFALLS

The practice guidelines provided above cover nearly every major ethical dilemma you will face as a case manager. Nonetheless, there are several important and common ethical issues that should be emphasized since they can be particularly troublesome to both you and your clients. You may feel as though these issues will never apply to you; however, every year, many case managers who thought these principles were too obvious to deserve their attention lose their licenses or face legal action because they have behaved unethically. Do not let this be you. Take the time to pay particular attention to the following ethical hazards:

- *Never share information without permission.* Confidentiality is the first rule of any health care provider. This means that you can never share information about your clients with anyone, unless your clients give you explicit written permission. The rare exception to this rule is sharing information with other members of your organization who are directly involved in treating the client. Friends, colleagues, family members, and office managers should never be told about the status, diagnosis, and/or treatment of a client.

- *Never have sex or become personally intimate with your clients.* Relationships between clients and case managers can become very close over time, allowing the relationship to feel intimate. Some case managers and clients have difficulty maintaining the professional boundaries within such close relationships. If you cross these boundaries, you will no longer be helping your clients. A professional relationship involves a concentration on your client's needs and not your own. If you lose track of this principle, you will begin to contribute to your client's problems rather than helping solve them. You will compromise your ability to be helpful to this client and others. You should never become intimately involved with any client, past or present.

- *Never be dishonest with your clients.* As a new case manager, you may be tempted to provide false reassurance, inaccurate information, or inappropriate advice to protect your clients from realities that seem painful. Your intentions may be good, but your clients need to come to grips with their own reality. Chances are you will only be fooling yourself, since clients are usually acutely aware of dishonesty. You will very likely be

doing them a major disservice if they act on misleading information, and you will damage their trust in you. You should never
lie to your clients. The honesty involved in saying that you do
not know an answer to a question they have asked contributes
to the relationship's foundation of trust. You can offer to try to
find out what they want to know from a colleague, mentor, or
supervisor.

- *Do not encourage dependency.* Clients who need case management
  are at least minimally dependent on these services. If they were
  not at least temporarily vulnerable, you would not be needed.
  However, this does not mean you should do everything for clients. It might feel easier, but it is more important to help them
  learn the skills they need to do things for themselves. It is your
  responsibility to encourage as much independence and autonomy as possible since you will not be available to your clients
  forever. Work to expose people to the experiences and skills they
  need for independent functioning, providing only the critical
  services clients have yet to master.

- *Never coerce clients.* The individuals you serve will often be
  dependent on you for essential services and resources for living,
  which puts a fair amount of power in your hands and opens up
  the possibility of using this power for coercive purposes—for
  example, indicating that you will take your client to see a new
  housing program as long as he attends all his treatment groups.
  This seemingly benign statement is an example of a coercive
  ultimatum, because your client's right to live where he wants
  should not be jeopardized by his group attendance. You must be
  mindful of the power you hold to help your clients and be sure
  to review your decisions continually to ensure that this power
  has not been misused and turned into coercion.

❖ MANDATED REPORTING

There are some situations so severe that the No. 1 rule of confidentiality
can be broken. These situations include those where a person is a
reasonable threat to himself or herself or to others, or when you have
evidence that abuse or neglect is occurring. In such situations, a case
manager is a *mandated reporter,* in that she or he is required by law to
notify the police, psychiatrist, and/or child welfare agency of the
problem. The idea behind mandated reporting is simple: Confidentiality

can be broken when people's lives are at stake. If a client is a threat to him- or herself, it is acceptable to call the psychiatrist or hospital without obtaining permission from the client. In addition, if you have specific information that your client is planning to harm someone, you are actually obligated to break confidentiality. Your duty in such an instance would be to notify the police and warn the potential victim. This mandate was determined in an influential court case (*Tarasoff v. Regents of the University of California*) after Tarasoff, a college student, was murdered by a client in mental health care. Tarasoff was not warned by the treating professionals that the client had plans to harm her. You also are required by law to notify the local child welfare department if you have evidence that a client may be abusing or neglecting his or her children. Similarly, if your client is dependent on others (as is often the case) and those caretakers are abusing or neglecting him or her, you are required to notify the police. The common rule to follow in handling all situations in which someone is in immediate danger is to ensure his or her safety even if it requires you to break confidentiality.

Of course, even when you have to break confidentiality, you do not stop treating your client with dignity and respect. If at all possible, it is best to tell your client the reasons you must reveal his or her issues to a psychiatrist, the police, or a child welfare agency. If the psychiatrist is at your agency, it is likely he or she will already know of the client's problems and, therefore, confidentiality will not be broken. When your client is a danger to others, the law requires that you report him or her to the police or a child welfare agency, but you can continue to support your client through what is likely to be a very difficult situation. Finally, above all, you need to discuss any issue regarding mandated reporting with your supervisor, mentor, or the treatment team prior to taking action. This allows you to share this important responsibility with others, letting those with more experience participate in determining the best decision.

❖ PSYCHIATRIC ADVANCE DIRECTIVES

Your role as a case manager will open you up to a series of unique ethical dilemmas in which in-the-moment decisions can be difficult to make. One of the most common ethical dilemmas is how to proceed with a client who has lost his or her decision-making capacity. Clients will go through crises and experience recurrences of severe mental health symptoms. While you hope to minimize these situations, they will still occur and, at times, will be so serious that the client will not be able to make a safe decision on his or her own. For example, a client could have a severe recurrence of psychosis that makes her believe she should hurt herself to atone for her sins. This is obviously a problem that requires psychiatric care and likely hospital care, but she refuses treatment and insists that she will be fine once she washes herself of her sins. The ethical dilemma arises then: Who should make decisions for the client? Who knows best what the client would want? Should treatment be administered against her will? All these questions are difficult to answer without input from the client, but at this time the client cannot give input that will be in her best interest.

A psychiatric advance directive addresses the common issue faced by clients and case managers of what to do with psychiatric care in case the client is not capable of making a decision on his or her own. These directives are legally binding documents, completed when clients are well and in a clear state of mind, outlining what they would prefer and view as helpful as far as their mental health treatment in the event that they are not able to make decisions about such treatment. This document then helps you as a case manager address the ethical dilemmas of what to do when a client cannot tell you what to do. Common items included in a psychiatric advance directive are presented in Table 4.2. These items should be formulated collaboratively with the client, his or her family, and yourself, and should reflect the client's true wishes about his or her care. When developed effectively, an advance directive puts the client in control, even in situations where he or she is not able to make clear decisions.

Table 4.2   Components to Include in a Psychiatric Advance Directive

Component	Example
Symptoms of a crisis	• Refusing to leave the house • Sleeping all day
Treatment choices	• Preferred medication • Preferred hospital or clinic
Emergency contacts	• Family • Treatment team
Prevention methods	• Seeking support from providers when symptoms of a crisis occur • Keeping a routine sleeping schedule • Getting regular exercise
Instructions to staff	• Avoid restraint • Speak slowly and calmly to me • Keep stimulation to a minimum in the hospital

❖ WHAT TO DO WHEN YOU
DON'T KNOW WHAT TO DO

We have provided you with some concrete guidelines for handling ethical problems that can arise in case management, but not all the situations requiring a response from you will be clear-cut. In the real world of direct work with clients, you will sometimes be presented with situations in which you must make a decision that might not strictly follow these rules. When decisions require a quick response, it is usually best to follow the basic principles of practice and respond in ways that maintain professional boundaries. However, there will be times when your instincts tell you it may be appropriate to deviate from these principles in the best interest of your client. Your decision about how to handle such situations will depend on the client, the context, and how much time you have to decide what to do. For example, when a client gives you a generous gift, do you accept it or return it to the client? Or when a grateful client tries to hug you, do you respond or keep your distance? There are two general rules to guide you: what feels comfortable to you and the likely consequences you can anticipate for your client. Would accepting a hug feel too intimate, or is this a client who might misinterpret the meaning of a hug? If a hug would make you uncomfortable, then chances are you should avoid the encounter. On the other hand, if you think refusing a hug would cause a particular client to feel rejected, you may be able to explain the rules to your client as you find other ways to respond warmly.

However you respond, a general rule is that when interactions with a client have made you uncomfortable or you think they are ethically or morally ambiguous, you should discuss them with your supervisor or mentor. Just having the discussion will provide you with some distance from the event and some support in coming to an objective and appropriate way of responding. If together you decide that your response was not the most helpful one, it is good to remember that you will always have other chances to respond in ways that will meet your client's needs. You and your supervisor can develop a plan for discussing the issue with your client, for reinforcing more appropriate boundaries, or for heading off ethical dilemmas before they occur. You can count on gradually developing your skills in deciding when to stick to basic professional case management guidelines and when to be flexible.

5

Identifying and Managing the Symptoms of Severe Mental Illness

Severe mental illnesses are characterized by a diverse array of symptoms that are often serious, difficult to understand, and even more difficult to manage, both for those who experience such symptoms and for those of us trying to help them. Still, persons with severe mental illness have significant strengths they can use to build a better life in their community. The job of a case manager is to understand the limitations imposed by symptoms, identify existing strengths, and work with a recovery orientation. This means your clients should always be provided with information about their illness, be encouraged to participate in plans for their community living, and be active participants in setting their own goals and decisions about treatment. Working with a recovery orientation, however, also requires that you know that these individuals may have spent years struggling with the symptoms of a debilitating illness, or even years in an institution. Clients have told us it is important that you understand what they have been through so you can understand how far they have come. They want you to appreciate what it has taken for them to get a handle on their symptoms and what it might take for them to continue to move toward recovery.

This chapter provides an overview of how to identify the most common classes of symptoms of severe mental illness (psychotic, mood, and personality), as well as some pragmatic strategies that can be used to manage them. Medication will be an important part of any of these strategies and is discussed in more detail in Chapter 6.

❖ IT'S NOT ALL ABOUT SYMPTOMS

Prior to embarking on a discussion of the common symptoms of severe mental illness, it is first important to note that people are not the symptoms they experience. No one is "schizophrenic," but there are people who experience the illness and symptoms of schizophrenia. No one is "bipolar," but some people may be coping with the illness of bipolar disorder. The distinction we are making may not sound that important, but it is crucial to remember that persons with mental illness are much more than the symptoms they experience; even those with long-term serious problems also have strengths. Your clients will have dreams, desires, goals, and likes and dislikes, just like you.

Over the years their illness may have caused them to become estranged from their family or friends, but they were once a part of a caring network of people who may be an invisible resource. Often alienation has occurred because family and friends did not understand or were frightened by their behaviors. Helping consumers reach out to this network and providing the network with information about the illness are just some of the ways of reintegrating clients into the community. The overall theme to remember is that however severe the illness has been and however long it has existed, your client is very likely to have available internal strengths and resources within the community that can be mobilized to help in the process of recovery.

❖ SYMPTOMS OF PSYCHOTIC DISORDERS

Spotting Psychosis

Psychotic disorders consist primarily of the group of schizophrenias. This group includes schizophrenia, schizoaffective disorder, schizophreniform disorder, delusional disorder, and shared psychotic disorder. The most common by far are schizophrenia and schizoaffective disorder (which is just like schizophrenia but also consists of prominent problems with mood [e.g., depression and/or anxiety]). Psychotic disorders contain a constellation of symptoms that may include

- *Hallucinations*—hearing, seeing, smelling, or feeling things that are not there;

- *Delusions*—firm beliefs (which are usually odd) that persist in spite of contradictory or available evidence;

- *Disorganized speech*—speech that does not make sense or frequently jumps from one idea to another;

- *Restricted affect and/or speech*—showing little emotion and/or speaking in only one- or two-word answers; and

- *Lack of motivation*—difficulty initiating and following through with goals and plans.

The unusual nature of most symptoms of psychosis makes them relatively easy to spot even if the person does not specifically share them with you. Persons experiencing *hallucinations* may appear to be reacting to something that is not there, may point or laugh inappropriately, may engage in conversation with themselves (i.e., self-talk), or may tell you about uncomfortable and peculiar feelings (e.g., bugs crawling under their skin). By far the most common symptoms of acute schizophrenia involve hallucinations—that is, hearing voices or seeing people or things that are not present. As individuals experience these symptoms they will react in ways that seem inappropriate to the rest of the world. For example, a person hearing a blaming or condescending voice may shout, "Stop it!" when no one else has heard a thing. You can just imagine how disturbing it might be to see or hear things others do not, especially if these visions or voices involve threatening or negative things. Your clients may become fearful and avoid contact with the world as a way of trying to control the environment they perceive.

Delusions are often most identifiable by odd or eccentric behavior displayed by clients (e.g., fearful avoidance of windows, wearing a foil antenna hat) or by direct discussion of bizarre beliefs (e.g., that they are being controlled by a computer, that they are God, that they are radioactive). Those individuals experiencing general delusions often will be willing to discuss them readily with you. However, paranoid delusions (i.e., that people are against them, spying on them, etc.) are usually identifiable only through bizarre behavior, since clients who have them are often unlikely to trust you enough to share them.

Paranoid delusions are particularly problematic for those people who experience them, in part because they are less responsive to medication. Over time, clients' delusions come to dominate their lives, causing increased isolation because they trust no one.

Disorganized speech is easily identifiable through conversation. A person will appear to be speaking gibberish or jumping quickly from topic to topic with very loose associations (e.g., "I need to take a shower. My friend is having a baby this month. I can't wait for Thanksgiving."). If you work hard, you might be able to make a connection between taking a shower and the likely baby shower, but fitting these associations with anticipating Thanksgiving would not only require a pretty extreme stretch but would also not be very helpful.

Restricted affect and/or speech and a *lack of motivation* are a few of the known "negative" symptoms of psychotic illnesses. People with psychosis, particularly when they are not experiencing an acute episode (e.g., severe and frequent hallucinations), will often go through an extended period of severe inactivity. They may respond to questions in one or two words, show little emotional expression on their faces, and have difficulty in "getting going." Some will sleep most of the day, some will have no interest in things they once cared about, and others will simply have no enthusiasm for anything. While these symptoms are not terribly difficult to spot, other people often fail to see them as a legitimate part of the illness. For example, when a person with a psychotic disorder does not follow through on the goals she sets, both professionals and loved ones often think this is due to laziness or resistance. It is very hard to watch someone just vegetate her life away. In fact, many family members tell us that before they understood the illness, these behaviors were more difficult to tolerate than the acute psychotic phase of the disorder. Additionally, people around those with such symptoms may think they are rude since they can be so unresponsive. Remember, these symptoms are part of the disease of psychosis and cannot merely be willed away.

As a case manager, the clients you will see may be experiencing negative symptoms of the illness that sometimes last for months and even years. While there are medications to help persons have some control over hallucinations, delusions, and disorganized speech, medications often do not alleviate negative symptoms. And, of course, medications often do not totally eliminate hallucinations and delusions, so you can expect that some of the individuals you serve may continue to experience delusions or less disruptive hallucinations even when taking medication.

Tips for Working With Individuals Who Are Experiencing Psychosis

There are some good rules of thumb for working with a person who has symptoms of a psychotic disorder. Three general pieces of advice are as follows:

- *Do not overreact to or challenge psychotic symptoms.* It is often extremely disturbing to see a person behave in ways that are acutely psychotic, and new case managers may be frightened by the symptoms they see. It is important not to add stress to the situation by becoming fearful or agitated yourself. Think of how hard it must be for the individual experiencing these symptoms. You can best help by not directly challenging the person's beliefs. Do not tell her that there are no voices or that what she sees is not there. It is far more comforting to move to another topic or listen and empathize about how hard it must be to believe she sees or hears these upsetting things. If these symptoms are chronic, you can best help by discussing how to manage these symptoms (most consumers who have been ill for a long time have some pretty good ideas of how to cope with the voices or the delusions, at least temporarily). If a client reports hearing voices or experiences that are new, you should do your best to get her to her psychiatrist for a reevaluation of her medication.

- *Push for change but not rapid change.* Psychotic disorders are very severe mental illnesses that take a long time to get better, but eventually the time between episodes can be lengthened and in many cases the illness can become significantly less problematic over time. It is important that you appreciate the need for a gradual process of change, helping clients move slowly and steadily through the successive achievement of small, manageable goals. It is equally important that you not get frustrated with slow progress and give up any hope for change. Working with your clients to set realistic goals will also preserve your own mental health.

- *Assess the risk of harm to self or others.* People often think that suicide is primarily associated with depression, but persons with psychotic disorders are also at an enhanced risk for attempting and completing suicide. You should always take suicidal thoughts, threats, or actions seriously. Assess your client for the risk of suicide if you have any indication that there is a serious decrease in functioning or mood. Once you have established a trusting relationship with the client, asking about suicidal thoughts and plans can be an effective way for assessing this risk. Harm to others is not as common as the media might suggest, but it is also something you will want to assess, especially if your client has harmed people in the past or has expressed views that a particular person has caused him or her harm in some way. If you sense imminent danger, give the person space, protect yourself, and get help.

❖ SYMPTOMS OF MOOD DISORDERS

Spotting Depression and Mania

There are several types of mood disorders: major depressive disorder, bipolar disorder, dysthymic disorder, and cyclothymic disorder. All of these have the common symptoms of very low moods (i.e., depression) or very high moods (i.e., mania and hypomania). Some mood disorders (bipolar) move from one extreme in mood and activity to the other. The two types of mood disorders you are most likely to encounter as a case manager are major depressive disorder and bipolar disorder. The primary symptoms of such disorders include the following:

- *Depression*—feeling sad, frequent crying, extreme irritability, complaints of feeling hopeless or worthless, having thoughts of suicide

- *Mania*—inflated self-esteem, grandiose plans, excess energy, excessive spending or sexual behavior, racing thoughts

Seeing *depression* as a serious illness can sometimes be difficult because everyone can feel "blue" from time to time. However, when someone feels down and hopeless for weeks on end and these feelings are severe enough to disrupt biological functioning (e.g., sleep, appetite, sex drive) or psychosocial functioning (e.g., work, school, relationships), it is a good indication that they have major depressive disorder. When a low mood state goes on for prolonged periods but is not severe enough to meet the criteria we just described for major depressive disorder, the condition is called dysthymia, a chronic low-grade low mood. Sometimes people have what is called "double depression," which involves a major depressive disorder on top of a long history of dysthymia. In case management, you will probably only be assigned people with mood disorders that are very serious and chronic. These individuals may express feelings of sadness or guilt; have significant changes in sleep, appetite, sexual interest, or the ability to work; have poor interpersonal relationships; or have difficulty carrying out the normal tasks of daily life. Individuals experiencing depression often tend to have suicidal thoughts and may be at *substantial risk for committing suicide.* Assessing for this risk and coming up with a plan of action are discussed in detail in Chapter 8.

Mania is not usually difficult to spot, as the behavior of individuals experiencing such symptoms tends to be extreme. People experiencing mania will often appear to be very excited and may seem to be speaking "a mile a minute." Such individuals will often have substantial difficulty sitting still or staying on a single train of thought, have little need for sleep, and have "big" or grandiose ideas and unrealistic plans. They may spend excessive amounts of money, engage in sexual activity with multiple partners, and appear to have both impaired judgment and limitless energy. Sometimes these symptoms of mania can be so severe that they emerge as psychosis. Suicide is also a risk for individuals with mania, especially when judgment is impaired or someone who is manic senses the impending shift to depression.

Tips for Working With Individuals Who Are Experiencing Depression or Mania

There are some good rules of thumb for working with individuals who are experiencing acute episodes of depression or mania. Three of the most important ones include the following:

- *Remember that you are part of a team.* The symptoms of serious mental illness are not just your responsibility. If you notice subtle or dramatic changes in how your client functions, take this information to your supervisor, mentor, and the team. They can help decide what interventions are necessary.

- *Remember that the symptoms are not willful.* The biggest problem new case managers might have in working with people with mood disorders is assuming the client could control the symptoms if he just tried hard enough. When working with an individual who has been depressed for a long time, a case manager may have the tendency to just want him to "snap out of it." It is important to remember that the individual would snap out of it if he could. Consequently, telling people with depression to cheer up is usually a fruitless endeavor that will only frustrate you and the people you are serving. When an individual is experiencing mania, there is often a tendency to underestimate his or her pain and become judgmental about the symptoms of the illness. Blatant or excessive sexual activity can be interpreted as immoral or illegal conduct rather than a symptom of illness. Excessive spending can seem like just bad planning. It is important to remember that these behaviors do not reflect the values of the person but are symptoms of an illness. It definitely will not help the person to order him or her to slow down or behave.

- *Keeping an eye on the potential for suicide.* Whether the problem is major depressive disorder or bipolar disorder, there is a risk of suicide. While the client with serious depression or mania will have a therapist who will be keeping tabs on this issue, your frequent contacts with the client may put you in a position to be more aware of changes in mental state than others on the team. If you have concerns about changes in a client's mood or behavior, it is reasonable and important to ask whether he has thoughts of harming himself. It is important to know that suicide does not occur just when someone is sad and despondent. In fact, sometimes when a depressed individual is starting to seem better, he is at greater risk because he has more energy or has made a decision. We cannot emphasize enough the importance of taking any questions you have about the significance of changes in client behaviors to your mentor, supervisor, or team.

❖ SYMPTOMS OF PERSONALITY DISORDERS

Spotting Personality Problems

Personality disorders consist of a wide mix of mental health problems that can emerge when someone has a persistent and pervasive abnormal way of seeing the world. These disorders are called "personality disorders" because they tend to permeate every aspect of daily life and thus are tied to a person's "personality." These clients are usually not directly out of touch with reality, but they can be seriously impaired. Because the symptoms of personality disorders are so varied, they tend to be clustered into different categories. For your purposes as a case manager, it is important to remember that the symptoms of some people with personality disorders involve so much impairment that they cannot maintain relationships and adequate functioning in the world. Some have seriously strange, distorted beliefs, self-destructive or antisocial behaviors, a narcissistic approach to relationships and the world, or totally incapacitating obsessive-compulsive rituals. Perhaps the most common personality disorder encountered by case managers is borderline personality disorder, which is characterized by a severe instability of relationships, affect, and self-esteem, as well as frequent suicidal gestures or self-harming behaviors.

Personality disorders can be difficult to diagnose and notoriously difficult to manage. While all of us tend to have some quirks in our personalities, individuals who have personality disorders sufficiently severe to end up in case management have "quirks" that cause serious problems that never seem to recede. They have lives that are frequently in crisis, rituals that drive people away, and severe relationship difficulties, and tend to alienate those who try to help them. Some move from one partner to another or waver between love and hate within the same relationship, while others have a remarkable lack of interest in social relationships and the feelings of others. Some will have ideas about things in their lives becoming contaminated that will seem as "fixed" and unchangeable as delusions. People with personality disorders can test your patience and ability to maintain a helping relationship over time.

There are three categories of personality disorders listed in the current *Diagnostic and Statistical Manual of Mental Disorders* (4th edition, text revision). These include Clusters A, B, and C personality disorders. Common signs within each cluster are listed below. Note that all these signs and symptoms must be so pervasive as to touch on nearly all aspects of an individual's life and impair the ability to function effectively.

Cluster A (paranoid, schizoid, and schizotypal personality disorders):

- Persistent and pervasive distrust of others

- Persistent and pervasive social detachment

- Perceptual disturbances that do not meet full diagnostic criteria for psychosis

- "Magical" thinking not congruent with cultural or social norms

- Persistent and pervasive interpersonal challenges and difficulties

Cluster B (antisocial, borderline, histrionic, and narcissistic personality disorders):

- Emotionally callous behavior and disregard for the welfare of others

- Frequent legal difficulties and failure to adhere to rules and laws

- Markedly unstable interpersonal relationships

- Self-mutilation

- Impulsiveness

- Inflated sense of self

- Constant need to be the center of social attention

Cluster C (avoidant, dependent, and obsessive-compulsive personality disorders):

- Frequent social isolation and excessive fear of being disliked

- Pervasive need to be cared for by others

- Difficulty making decisions without excessive advice and reassurance

- Obsessive preoccupation with details, lists, and organization

- Ritualistic behavior

- Lack of cognitive flexibility

Tips for Working With Individuals With Personality Problems

Personality disorders are being increasingly recognized as a form of severe mental illness, and, thus, you will find yourself more frequently encountering in your practice individuals who experience these disorders. Some good rules of thumb for working with individuals who experience personality problems include the following:

- *Foster a helping relationship.* The relationship between you and a person experiencing personality problems is one of the most powerful tools you can use to help facilitate recovery, or at least help develop a life with less destructive symptoms. Being direct but genuine, friendly, and kind will go a long way toward developing a healthy helping relationship and succeeding with persons experiencing these problems. It is difficult to do, but the best way to manage your relationship with these individuals is to spend more time with them when they are not in crisis and less when they are.

- *Set clear limits.* Individuals with personality problems can have a tendency to cross professional boundaries and demand an excess of a case manager's time. You should always be very clear about your rules and stick to your professional boundaries (e.g., that you will not take phone calls on vacation). These limits will be seriously challenged, especially by those with borderline personality disorder. Because these clients can be so provocative and demanding, it is important to avoid falling into a pattern of overresponding and then becoming frustrated and rejecting. It is crucial that you not avoid clients when they are behaving well. To maintain a relationship with these clients and help them over the long run, they must learn that you will be more available when you are not provoked.

- *Maintain emotional stability.* Often individuals with personality problems will "press your buttons." They seem to know just what might bother you the most and do it artfully. Keeping your cool by not reacting emotionally when this happens will reduce the likelihood of such incidents happening again and again. Your response will serve as a reminder that you are a stable and committed person in their lives. For example, if a client is cursing at you and calling you the worst case manager in the world, it is appropriate to set a limit that this behavior is not acceptable. Rather than getting upset, remain calm and tell them that they can either get themselves under control now or you will return later when they have themselves together. If they have gotten you agitated, debrief with your colleagues rather than sharing your frustrations with the clients.

❖ HELPING CONSUMERS MANAGE SYMPTOMS OF SEVERE MENTAL ILLNESS

Although severe mental illnesses tend to differ with regard to their symptom presentations, there are a number of common strategies that can be shared with clients to help them manage their symptoms, regardless of the specific condition. The best of these strategies include a combination of the right medication (discussed in detail in Chapter 6) and self-protective techniques clients can use to reduce their vulnerability to stress.

Severe mental illness can be thought of as an extreme response to a heightened sensitivity to stimulation and stress. As can be seen by the *stress-vulnerability curve* presented in Figure 5.1, almost anyone could cross the threshold from being well to becoming ill if the life stressors they encounter became sufficiently extreme. However, most of us would need to experience very severe physical or environmental stresses to cross this line. People who experience a severe mental illness under ordinary circumstances probably have a greater biological or genetic vulnerability to stress, such that they require significantly fewer life stressors to cross the threshold from being well to becoming ill. Consequently, finding ongoing ways to decrease stress is crucial. It is important to remember that even what seem like positive life events can be sources of stress, such as getting a job, having a family member marry, getting out of the hospital, meeting someone for the first time on a date, and so on.

Figure 5.1   Stress-Vulnerability Curve

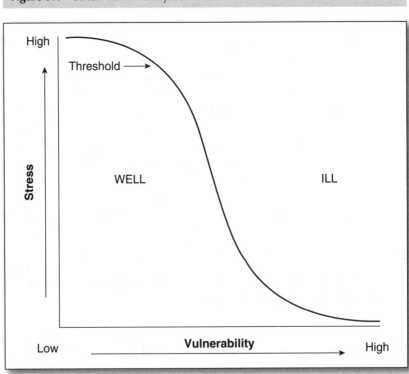

Source: Adapted from Anderson, Reiss, and Hogarty (1986).

Below we list just a few strategies for managing stress that might help you help your clients, in addition to their seeing their therapist or taking their medication.[1] If you work as part of a team, other strategies may arise from the group, and following the suggestions developed as part of the treatment plan is always a good idea.

- *Knowing the early signs of distress.* The exacerbation of the symptoms of severe mental illness often can be prevented by catching little stresses before they add up to big ones and by identifying early warning signs of impending distress so strategies can be used to address them. Some of these signs (e.g., sleep problems, pacing, restlessness, increased fears) are common for many individuals. Other signs that signal an acute episode can be specific to an individual (e.g., an increase in reading the Bible, excessive showering, increased isolation). Family members and the individuals themselves come to know these signs over the course of long-term illness, so often they can identify early signs for you so you both can plan some sort of action to avoid the development of a full-blown episode. A formal process for doing this through a Wellness Action and Recovery Plan will be discussed in Chapter 8.

- *Reducing stimulation.* Creating and reinforcing an environment with little stimulation (e.g., lots of people, noise, or even light) can also be very effective during times of increased stress. You can work with individuals to create a specific plan for managing what causes them to become overstimulated. Many will be able to identify the kinds of things that tend to set them off. If they cannot, it will be a process of trial and error, but the important thing is that everyone on the team helps by working with clients to create a list of ways to reduce stimulation temporarily as soon as clients first begin to feel overwhelmed.

- *Using distraction.* Some individuals find it helpful to be distracted from their symptoms, particularly individuals experiencing psychosis. Getting their minds off the voices they hear in their heads may offer some comfort or may even reassure them that they have at least a bit of control over these disturbing

---

[1]These strategies are taken largely from the book *Personal Therapy for Schizophrenia and Related Disorders: A Guide to Individualized Treatment,* by G. E. Hogarty (2002), which is highly recommended for those looking for more detail on methods of managing stress in psychosis and other severe mental illnesses.

occurrences. Some, for example, find it helpful to listen to music through a set of headphones to block out the voices.

- *Avoiding criticism.* Criticism is a normal part of life and relationships, but it can be particularly stressful for individuals with severe mental illness. You can help by maintaining a strengths focus and finding ways to send or interpret critical messages in a more positive way, and by helping those who live with the individual do the same.

6

Medications for Managing the Symptoms of Severe Mental Illness

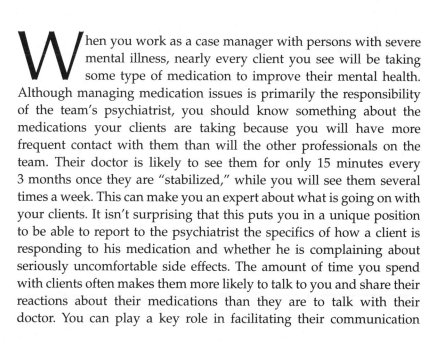

When you work as a case manager with persons with severe mental illness, nearly every client you see will be taking some type of medication to improve their mental health. Although managing medication issues is primarily the responsibility of the team's psychiatrist, you should know something about the medications your clients are taking because you will have more frequent contact with them than will the other professionals on the team. Their doctor is likely to see them for only 15 minutes every 3 months once they are "stabilized," while you will see them several times a week. This can make you an expert about what is going on with your clients. It isn't surprising that this puts you in a unique position to be able to report to the psychiatrist the specifics of how a client is responding to his medication and whether he is complaining about seriously uncomfortable side effects. The amount of time you spend with clients often makes them more likely to talk to you and share their reactions about their medications than they are to talk with their doctor. You can play a key role in facilitating their communication about possible negative reactions so they do not become so uncomfortable that they stop taking a medication that could otherwise be helpful in keeping them well.

While it is always best to help empower clients to learn about their medications so they can recognize the effects and side effects and convey this information to their psychiatrist on their own, your client may need a little help from you to get this conversation going or to clarify the details of what he or she may be experiencing. Consequently, while you should **NEVER** be responsible for making medical decisions about the medications people with severe mental illness take, it is of the utmost importance that you have some knowledge about these medications and their use. This chapter will outline the medications most commonly used to treat psychotic, mood, and personality disorders, as well as the more serious side effects that can arise from the use of such medications.

❖ MEDICATIONS FOR MANAGING PSYCHOTIC DISORDERS

The medications most commonly used to treat psychotic disorders are called *antipsychotic* or *neuroleptic* medications. These medicines are proven to reduce the hallucinations, delusions, and disorganized thinking that are a part of psychosis. These medications tend to begin working quickly, although it may take a few weeks or months for a client to experience their full impact. For most people, these medications not only reduce psychotic symptoms during an acute episode but also keep the symptoms of psychosis at bay over time. Some clients, and even friends or family members who care about them, question the value of taking these drugs. After the acute symptoms of psychosis have been brought under control, clients may abruptly stop taking their medication. When clients first stop taking their medication, they will look brighter and seem better. Unfortunately, neither you, the clients, nor their families will immediately appreciate the positive impact the medication has been having for some time, since antipsychotic medications stay in the body for several months after they have been discontinued. This delay in experiencing the impact of how these medicines have been helping can operate to deter adherence. When your clients stop their medication, they will initially feel better because the side effects diminish while the therapeutic effects remain. Inexperienced case managers might agree with them, noting their client's brighter affect, unaware of the negative impact that they will see a few months down the line. You can help your clients and their significant others by sharing information about how these medicines help, the delay in the benefits clients will receive from them, and the delayed negative impact of discontinuing them. If clients can be helped to see the real connection between taking medication and well-being, they will be much more supportive of their own medication program. Without this understanding, individuals are less likely to take their medication consistently, resulting in more frequent acute episodes, crises, and hospitalizations. Because each psychotic episode takes a toll, avoiding these events is crucial. Taking medication on a consistent basis provides important protection. Many clients with a psychotic disorder require antipsychotic medications, ideally in ever-diminishing amounts, for most of their lives. Some antipsychotic medicines are available in long-lasting injectable forms for those who have trouble taking pills every day.

Today, antipsychotic medications tend to be categorized into two different classes: first- and second-generation antipsychotics. The second-generation antipsychotics tend to be prescribed more but are not necessarily more effective (with the exception of Clozaril). Their difference is mainly in the potential side effects they can induce. Table 6.1 lists some of the first- and second-generation antipsychotic medications commonly prescribed to persons with psychotic disorders. You do not need to know each of these medications, but knowing the name and its therapeutic dose range will help you know what your clients are being treated for and how well.

Side Effects of Antipsychotic Medications

While antipsychotic medications have been remarkably effective at controlling some of the symptoms of psychotic disorders, they also have had a tendency to induce serious unwanted side effects. As mentioned above, first- and second-generation antipsychotics tend to have their own unique side effects, each of which can be very serious. First-generation antipsychotics can induce motor side effects that resemble symptoms of Parkinson's disease—that is, involuntary muscle and facial movements, extreme restlessness (akathisia), tremors, slowing of voluntary movements (akinesia), and/or muscle stiffness.

All these side effects can be serious for the people who experience them; however, the two most serious side effects of first-generation antipsychotics include *tardive dyskinesia* and *neuroleptic malignant syndrome*. These conditions, which can develop as a result of antipsychotic medication use, can be severe and permanent. Tardive dyskinesia is a potentially permanent condition exhibited by

Table 6.1 Antipsychotic Medications Used for Treating Psychosis

Common Name	Medical Name
First-generation antipsychotics	
Haldol*	Haloperidol
Loxitane	Loxapine
Mellaril	Thioridazine
Moban	Molindone
Navane	Thiothixene
Prolixin*	Fluphenazine
Serentil	Mesoridazine
Stelezine	Trifluoperazine
Thorazine	Chlorpromazine
Trilafon	Perphenazine
Second-generation antipsychotics	
Abilify	Aripiprazole
Clozaril	Clozapine
Risperidal*	Risperidone
Seroquel	Quetapine
Geodon	Ziprasidone HCL
Zyprexa	Olanzapine

*Available in long-lasting injectable (depot) form

involuntary movements in the upper extremities, particularly movements of the tongue, face, jaw, and/or lips. Clients who experience tardive dyskinesia may appear to be constantly smacking their lips or pushing out their tongues. If you note such symptoms, you should absolutely inform your client's psychiatrist. Neuroleptic malignant syndrome is a potentially fatal condition exhibited by fever and extreme muscle rigidity (e.g., trouble bending arms, legs, and/or back; feeling stiff as a board). This is a rare side effect, and chances are physicians would know about it, but just in case they do not, if you observe such symptoms you should tell your supervisor and/or the team about your concerns immediately so your client can be seen by a physician as soon as possible.

Second-generation antipsychotic medications only rarely induce the motor side effects seen in first-generation drugs (although they do sometimes, so keep your eye out for them). However, they do have a tendency to produce adverse effects on the metabolic system in the forms of *increased body weight, high cholesterol, high blood pressure*, and/or *insulin resistance.* In some severe cases, these side effects can lead to diabetes, stroke, or heart attack. Consequently, making sure the medical team is monitoring such side effects through routine weight and blood measurements is vital to ensuring the safety of individuals taking these second-generation antipsychotics. Significant weight gain after starting a new antipsychotic is one of the best signs that these metabolic side effects are forming as a result of the drug. While it is not your responsibility to monitor your client's medical condition, if you do notice a sign such as sudden substantial weight gain, it is important you notify your supervisor and work to help the client see his or her physician so the possibility of antipsychotic-induced metabolic side effects can be explored.

In addition to various metabolic side effects, the second-generation antipsychotic Clozaril carries with it the rare possibility of agranulocytosis, a dangerous reduction in white blood cells. Although the condition is rare, because of this potentially fatal side effect, everyone taking Clozaril should have routine blood work done biweekly or at least monthly. This may seem inconvenient to many individuals, but since Clozaril is really the only effective antipsychotic medication for psychotic symptoms resistant to other antipsychotics, the trouble is usually worth it for those clients who experience treatment-resistant psychosis. Nonetheless, since this particular medication can have such a severe side effect, if you serve a client who is taking Clozaril without receiving frequent blood draws, lobbying for an immediate appointment with a physician is called for.

❖ MEDICATIONS FOR MANAGING MOOD DISORDERS

Antidepressant Medications

The medications most commonly used for treating depressive disorders include the classes of drugs known as antidepressants. Four major classes of antidepressants exist: tricyclic antidepressants, monoamine oxidase inhibitors, selective serotonin reuptake inhibitors, and a group of new atypical antidepressants. Most antidepressant medications work on the serotonin neurotransmitter system in the brain, and all have been shown effective at improving depressed mood and relieving anxiety. Tricyclic antidepressants (e.g., Elavil) and monoamine oxidase inhibitors (e.g., Nardil) are older medications and have been largely abandoned for newer selective serotonin reuptake inhibitors and atypical antidepressants, as these newer drugs tend to be safer, work faster, and have fewer serious side effects. However, these older drugs are still prescribed if the newer selective serotonin reuptake inhibitors and atypical antidepressants are not effective for a specific client.

Regardless of the type of antidepressant medication used, all these drugs can take from 2 weeks to 2 months before individuals start feeling improvement in their depression. While older antidepressant medications tend to take longer to work, even the newer drugs usually take at least 2 weeks before a person starts experiencing their benefits. It is critical that clients know how long it will take before they will see improvement from one of these drugs or they are likely to stop taking their antidepressant medication before it has actually had a chance to work, particularly if they experience the side effects before the beneficial effects. They should be encouraged to be patient and give the drug time to take effect. Antidepressants, like antipsychotic medications, stay in a person's system for some time after discontinuation, but repeatedly missing doses can dramatically reduce the therapeutic effects of these drugs, so consistency in taking them is still very important. Table 6.2 lists some of the most commonly prescribed antidepressant medications used to treat depression.

Side Effects of Antidepressant Medications

The many different kinds of antidepressants that exist for treating depressive symptoms can bring forth a large array of side effects. While most of these side effects are not terribly serious, they can be quite annoying for clients. Common side effects associated with antidepressant medications include *sexual dysfunction* (e.g., impotence, lack of sexual interest), *weight gain, headaches, dry mouth, sensitivity to light, diarrhea,* and *nausea.* While none of these side effects is particularly serious or life threatening, many clients will complain about weight gain and loss of interest in sex. These problems certainly can influence their appearance and their relationships, often causing clients to discontinue their medication even if it has helped their depression. You can help by suggesting they ask their nurse or psychiatrist about potential alternative medications (of which there are many, as shown in

Table 6.2   Antidepressant Medications Used for Treating Depression

Common Name	Medical Name
Atypical antidepressants	
Desyrel	Trazodone
Effexor	Venlafaxine
Remeron	Mirtazapine
Serzone	Nefazodone
Wellbutrin	Bupropion
Selective serotonin reuptake inhibitors	
Celexa	Citalopram
Lexapro	Escitalopram
Luvox*	Fluvoxamine
Paxil	Paroxetine
Prozac*	Fluoxetine
Zoloft	Sertraline
Tricyclic antidepressants	
Adapin	Doxepin
Anafranil	Clomipramine
Elavil	Amitriptyline
Norpramin	Desipramine
Pamelor	Nortriptyline
Surmontil	Trimipramine
Tofranil	Imipramine
Vivactil	Protriptyline
Monoamine oxidase inhibitors	
Nardil	Phenelzine
Parnate	Tranylcypromine

*Also used to treat anxiety problems

Table 6.2). While most of the side effects of antidepressants are not severe, some are. Because some side effects can cause serious health problems, they are best monitored by physicians and nurses, and questions about uncomfortable responses to specific medications are best referred to those members of the team. Your primary responsibility in this area is to make sure your clients who are taking any medication are being seen by a physician on a regular basis and are reporting their reactions. You can help them make the best use of these appointments by helping them make a list of questions they can bring when it is time to see the doctor.

Mood-Stabilizing Medications

The category of mood disorders also includes disorders such as mania and bipolar disorder. Unfortunately, antidepressant medications have little beneficial effects on the symptoms of mania and can even cause a person who is prone to mania to experience manic symptoms. Consequently, bipolar disorder is treated with different medications from those used with major depression or dysthymic disorder. The most common medications used for treating bipolar disorder are the mood stabilizers and second-generation antipsychotic medications. Compared with other psychiatric medications, there are remarkably few mood stabilizers, and all but Lithium are anticonvulsants that are also used to treat seizure disorders. These medications are most effective at reducing symptoms of mania and the back-and-forth mood fluctuations between mania and depression seen in bipolar disorder. In addition, they are not terribly effective at reducing depressive symptoms. Like antidepressants, mood stabilizers can take several weeks to yield significant beneficial effects. Table 6.3 lists current mood-stabilizing medications used to treat bipolar disorder and other disorders that include manic symptoms and/or mood swings.

Side Effects of Mood-Stabilizing Medications

Mood stabilizers can carry with them all the minor side effects seen with antidepressants, such as sexual dysfunction, weight gain, hand tremors, nausea, and so on. Some mood stabilizers can also produce more serious side effects. For example, the difference between a therapeutic and toxic dose of Lithium is quite small and depends on one's body chemistry. Because of the high risk of toxic doses of Lithium when taking the drug, blood levels are usually monitored monthly to ensure Lithium in the body is at safe and therapeutic levels. Toxic doses of Lithium are very serious, and if your client who is taking Lithium

Table 6.3   Mood-Stabilizing Medications Used for Treating Mania and Bipolar Disorder

Common Name	Medical Name
Depacon	Sodium valproate
Depakene	Valproic acid
Depakote	Divalproex sodium
Lamictal	Lamotrigine
Lithium	Lithium carbonate
Neurontin	Gabapentin
Tegretol	Carbamazepine
Topamax	Topiramate
Trileptal	Oxcarbazepine

complains to you about *visual impairment, seizures, slurred speech, rapid or slow heart beat, trouble walking downstairs,* or *trouble keeping his or her balance,* an appointment with a physician should be scheduled immediately and your supervisor contacted. Likewise, medications such as Depacon, Depakene, Depakote, and Tegretol should also be monitored by monthly blood work because they can interfere with liver function and white blood cell production. If you have clients who are taking any of these medications and not receiving regular blood work from a physician, you should try to schedule them to see a doctor.

❖ MEDICATIONS FOR MANAGING PERSONALITY DISORDERS

Little to no existing medications are approved for treating personality disorders *per se*, and the most common treatments for comprehensively addressing the symptoms of these disorders primarily involve some form of psychotherapy, such as dialectical behavior therapy. Nonetheless, many of the medications discussed above are used as adjunctive treatments to address some of the emotional and behavioral problems that accompany personality disorders. Remember that many personality disorders include difficulty regulating emotion and mood, are often characterized by impulsive behaviors, and can present with symptoms of irritability and aggression. The current standard for the treatment of personality disorders with medications is to target medications to the specific emotional and behavioral symptoms someone with a personality disorder is experiencing. For persons experiencing depressed moods or anxiety, antidepressant medications are often prescribed. For those experiencing frequent mood swings, mood stabilizers are often used, even though these mood swings may not meet full diagnostic criteria for depressed or manic mood states. Both antidepressants and mood stabilizers have been used to treat impulsivity and aggression, but when these symptoms are severe enough, antipsychotic medications are sometimes used.

As you can see, the pharmacological management of personality disorder symptoms consists of a medley of medications designed to treat other disorders. This is partly the case because personality disorders frequently co-occur with mood and anxiety disorders, so psychiatrists must work on managing the symptoms of both disorders at the same time. In addition, relative to schizophrenia and depression, personality disorders have only recently been recognized as legitimate psychiatric illnesses in need of medical treatment. Consequently, far fewer treatment options exist for individuals experiencing personality disorder symptoms, and, currently, individuals suffering from these disorders must make do with whatever psychiatrists can pull together from their array of medicines used to treat other conditions. This highlights the importance of utilizing a combination of available treatment options for personality disorders, particularly psychotherapy, in addition to medication. Combined treatments often offer individuals with personality problems significant relief from their symptoms.

Let us emphasize again that it is not your responsibility as a case manager to manage or monitor your client's medication. We present this information so you can become familiar with the basic classes of medications and have intelligent conversations about medication with the team and your clients, supporting them when they experience difficult side effects. We hope you might be able to answer their general questions, but you should be prepared to refer your clients to the medical professionals on the team or to their primary care physician for any issues of serious concern.

❖ ENHANCING MEDICATION USE

One of the biggest problems regarding the use of medications to treat the symptoms of serious mental illness is that clients often have difficulty taking these medications consistently. There are a number of reasons for this. As discussed above, many of these medications have significant side effects, and clients often would rather experience the symptoms of severe mental illness than the side effects of the medications used to treat those symptoms. In addition to side effects, clients are often prescribed an array of medications that must be taken several times a day. Just as people without psychiatric disabilities have difficulty remembering to take their antibiotics when they are sick, individuals with severe mental illness often have difficulty remembering what medications to take and when, in part because of the marked impairments in thinking that can accompany these disorders. Further, it is natural for human beings to dislike taking medication, and individuals with severe mental illness are no exception to this rule. Some individuals have difficulty accepting that they have a mental disability, and others are merely dismayed by the thought that they may have to take medicine for the rest of their lives. The bottom line is that most people, whether they have a psychiatric disability or not, don't like taking medicine. However, we know it is vital that psychiatric medications be taken consistently, especially in psychosis, if they are to provide any relief from the symptoms people experience. As a case manager, you can do a number of things to help facilitate the consistency with which clients use their medication:

- *Help them use concrete medication supports.* Pill boxes and medication timers can take a lot of the work out of remembering what to take when.

- *Help them connect medication with daily routines.* Placing medication use within the context of daily routines is the way most people remember to take their medicine. For example, taking medicine with a morning cup of coffee is a good way to integrate medicine into existing daily activities.

- *Provide them with education about medications.* People don't take what they think doesn't work, or they stop taking a drug when they don't see the purpose of it. Education about what different drugs do can help.

- *Empathize with the difficulty of taking medications.* A great way to support medication use is to acknowledge the difficulty in being consistent, particularly in the face of side effects. Having support in the difficult task of taking medicine can help keep a person motivated.

- *Facilitate communication with the psychiatrist.* Helping clients communicate with their doctors when they feel a medicine is not working or when it is causing side effects is important for getting the right medication regime in place and for maximizing the benefits and minimizing the problems associated with medication use.

❖ SHARED DECISION MAKING REGARDING MEDICATIONS

Many case managers mistakenly believe that medication choice is a one-sided decision determined only by the psychiatrist. The psychiatrist is certainly a key contributor to decisions about medication, given the extensive training physicians receive on the efficacy, side effects, and health impact of medications. However, it is important that patients have a say in their medication regime. The best medication plans for psychiatric treatment involve a collaboration between the doctor and patient and, thus, a shared decision-making process about what to take, when, and how much. The basic decision about taking medicine is not usually totally negotiable, as medication is frequently a required cornerstone of effective mental health treatment. Beyond needing to take medication, many decisions must be made, and your client should be at the table for every single one of them.

A seemingly infinite number of psychotropic medications are now available for different mental health conditions, and they all work differently for different people. The doctor may know what is best in terms of overall effectiveness, but only your client can say what is working well for him. Recent studies have shown that more than 50% of clients discontinue their medication in the first year of treatment because of perceived ineffectiveness or side effects. Clearly, a medication plan that does not take into account what will work best for the client is likely doomed to fail. Even further, decisions about when to take medications and how frequently to take them are critical for many individuals, and they should be involved in this process. Psychotropic medications commonly produce fatigue and tiredness, and so many individuals would prefer to take them only once a day, in the evening. With the right dosage schedule this is often feasible, but it's something not likely to be considered unless the client is helping drive the decision making about medication use. Even medication dosage is negotiable and should involve input from the client, as effective dosing can be highly individualized depending on the physical characteristics of the individual. As a case manager, it will be important for you to educate your clients about their medicine so they can truly participate in shared decision making regarding medication treatment with the psychiatrist and the rest of the treatment team.

7

Resource Brokering

The Big Two

Asubstantial amount of case management time is involved in tracking down resources and setting up these resources so clients can use them. As discussed in Chapter 2, resource brokering is one of the primary responsibilities of the case manager. The resources case managers can call on to support the recovery of their clients are many and range from facilitating government disability payments to helping clients connect with peer companions. Furthermore, the location and logistics of attaining these resources tend to vary significantly by state, county, and even city. This makes it particularly difficult to transmit general knowledge to new case managers about how to locate and broker resources for their clients. Admittedly, much of this information would be dated as soon as it was written down on paper, and knowledge of different resources usually must be gleaned on a learn-as-you-go basis. There are, nonetheless, two major resources that every individual with severe mental illness is entitled to and likely to need. These resources relate to disability payments and benefits (usually in the form of Social Security, Medicaid, and/or Medicare). These benefits can provide clients with enough money to live, adequate access to health care, and housing options to ensure that such individuals have a place to call home. Fortunately, since these two important resources are federally administered, the general process of attaining them tends to be consistent across place and individual programs, although specifics can vary. This chapter will focus on providing a practical overview of how to locate, apply for, and attain housing and disability benefits for clients.

We have encouraged a strength-based recovery orientation. It is ironic that to obtain needed benefits, your clients must now prove not only that they are disabled but that they are likely to remain so. There is no getting around the fact that this is inconsistent. If your clients have a chance to become truly independent, they need these disability benefits to provide them with the safety net of stability, at least temporarily. They need a chance to use their energies to learn to manage their illness, develop work and social skills, and achieve their very best level of functioning.

❖ OVERVIEW OF DISABILITY BENEFITS

Many individuals with severe mental illness experience times when they are unable to work. This means they will have little to no income, and they are therefore entitled to financial support from the government in the form of disability benefits. The primary government body that administers disability benefits, whether they are due to mental or physical health problems, is the Social Security Administration (www .ssa.gov). This federal agency is responsible for distributing two types of disability benefits relevant to persons with severe mental illness. The first type is called Supplemental Security Income (SSI) and is available for persons who may never have worked and, therefore, never paid into the U.S. Social Security system. The second type is called Social Security Disability Insurance (SSDI) and is available for individuals who have worked a certain amount of time during the entire course of their employment tenure in all official jobs in the United States. The amount of time a person must have worked depends on his or her age at the time he or she became disabled and currently ranges from about 1.5 years for a 24-year-old to 9.5 years for a 60-year-old (Social Security Administration, 2011).[1] The primary difference between these two types of disability benefits, other than their eligibility criteria, is that SSDI tends to pay more than SSI because the system is designed to provide an advantage to people who have worked.

---

[1]This figure changes every year. Updated figures can be found at www.ssa .gov/pubs/10029.html.

Finally, the third type of disability benefit administered by the Social Security Administration is *Medicare,* which provides some (though not all) health care coverage for persons with psychiatric disabilities. Persons under 65 receiving SSI or SSDI are automatically enrolled in Medicare 2 years after they begin receiving benefits. This means that from the time clients start receiving SSI/SSDI until 2 years later, they need some other form of health insurance. In addition, since Medicare does not cover all health care needs, an additional form of health insurance is almost always needed. For individuals with psychiatric and other disabilities, this additional insurance comes from *Medicaid,* which is a state-operated, comprehensive health insurance program for individuals living in poverty. All these benefits, whether SSI/SSDI, Medicare, or Medicaid, require that individuals have a very low level of income, which usually precludes any full-time work (see Chapter 11 on employment for ways to deal with this problem).

❖ APPLYING FOR DISABILITY BENEFITS

The logistics of applying for Social Security benefits, whether SSI or SSDI, have been simplified over the years, and applications can now be submitted electronically on the World Wide Web, at www.ssa.gov/applyforbenefits, or through the toll-free number 1-800-772-1213 (1-800-325-0778 for TTY for individuals with hearing problems). Although technology now makes applying for Social Security benefits more convenient, the process is not so easy and is sometimes made intentionally difficult to deter some individuals from applying to receive benefits. Nevertheless, individuals with severe mental illnesses who cannot work are entitled to disability benefits from Social Security. The client must make a case for why he or she is disabled, and you as the case manager are really the facilitator of assembling this proof. The first step in applying for disability benefits is gathering information regarding the disability and the person's inability to work. This means collecting mental health diagnostic and assessment information, work history, and usually a doctor's note stating that the person is unable to work because of his or her disability. The case must also be made that the person is not only currently disabled but likely to be disabled for a long time to come. This can be shown by charting the history of a person's illness if his or her functioning has already been impaired for some time or by noting its severity. Regardless, Social Security will require you to submit a set of documents containing this information to prove your client is disabled.

After completing the application and submitting disability information, a phone or in-person interview at the local Social Security office is usually requested to go over the disability information. Both you and your client will need to be at this meeting, and you will need to prepare your case ahead of time to ensure you have all the information discussed above. Work history, diagnosis, and current symptoms are probably the most important pieces of information to have on hand, since they will help provide the strongest proof of disability. If for some reason the client is already receiving Medicaid and/or food stamps from the state, this will strongly support an application for Social Security. After the interview, the waiting game can take several months, and you may be requested to submit more information. Keep in regular (monthly) contact with the Social Security caseworker assigned to the case, and quickly submit any requested information to keep the application moving through the pipeline.

Having applied for Social Security disability benefits to ensure the client has some income, you will need to turn your attention to health insurance benefits. Medicare will usually be out of the question because new clients will likely be under 65 and will not have been receiving SSI/SSDI for 2 years. This means you will have to go through the state system to apply for Medicaid, which can also be quite difficult. The bad news is that this process can vary substantially from state to state. The good news is that all the information you assembled for the SSI/SSDI application can be used for the Medicaid application. State Medicaid programs are usually administered through state departments or offices such as the Department of Public Welfare, Office of Health and Human Services, or Department of Health Services. The name tends to differ with each state as well, but contact information for your specific state can be found at www.cms.hhs.gov/apps/contacts.

Once you have located the name and number of the department/office that runs the Medicaid program in your state, you can contact them to get information about your local city office, where you will most likely need to go in person with your client to apply for benefits. Be sure to bring everything you used for your client's Social Security application with you, in case the caseworker assigned to your client needs some of that documentation. At this time you can also usually submit an application for food stamps, which you should do jointly with the Medicaid application (some states include food stamps in Medicaid). After completing the initial application, you will again be waiting for a response or request for more information, which means you should stay in regular (monthly) contact with the caseworker to keep the application process moving. If at any time during your wait for approval for

Medicaid you receive approval for SSI/SSDI, you should contact the caseworker immediately, as the Medicaid office will automatically approve your client's application for Medicaid after receiving this information. While waiting for all these benefits, your client will usually need some form of income, so be sure to ask your mentor, supervisor, and other case managers what types of temporary income supports are available in your city and/or county. Most places provide some temporary income supports for people with disabilities who have submitted a Social Security application, with the understanding that any money given to the individual will be paid back once Social Security benefits, which can be paid retroactively, are granted.

❖ OVERVIEW OF HOUSING BENEFITS

Now that you have the ball rolling on income and health benefits that will help your client survive and receive adequate health care, you will most likely need to start working with your client to figure out a good living situation. Some clients may have made living arrangements before being discharged from the hospital, but in most cases these arrangements will be left to you. Some clients may be living with family members and may prefer to continue doing so.[2] Other clients may be temporarily without housing while arrangements are made for them to move into a housing or treatment facility, such as a group home. However, there will certainly be other clients who do not need to live in a treatment facility and do not currently have a stable place to live. As their case manager, you will need to begin linking them to available apartments or other community resources designed to help them find housing.

While different cities may offer different housing resources, the primary housing resource for persons with disabilities throughout the country is the *Section 8* program, operated by the federal Department of Housing and Urban Development (HUD). Section 8, named after the section of the Public Housing Act that defines the program, is a voucher-based housing program that provides individuals in poverty with additional money to rent public housing. The program works by paying a certain percentage of a person's rent, based on his or her income level (including SSI/SSDI), so that housing is affordable for everyone, regardless of income.

---

[2]If a client's family home is going to be the placement of choice, it will be important to connect family members with programs that will help them understand the illness and its treatment and to provide support to them in the process.

There are two types of Section 8 programs, which vary in availability by state. These include project-based and tenant-based programs. *Project-based* programs are those Section 8 programs that allow individuals to live where the government has built specific public housing. *Tenant-based* programs allow individuals to live anywhere they choose, as long as the landlord of the housing complex accepts Section 8 vouchers. Unfortunately, many landlords do not accept these vouchers, so individuals participating in tenant-based programs usually have somewhat restricted housing options. In addition, because Section 8 housing is available to anyone living in poverty and because the number of people who can receive Section 8 vouchers at any given time is limited, the waiting list is extraordinarily long, sometimes taking 3 to 5 years. Although the program is administered at the federal level, eligibility criteria vary from state to state and are tied to income level, not disability. Generally, individuals who earn less than 50% of the median income in their county are eligible for Section 8 housing benefits.

❖ APPLYING FOR HOUSING BENEFITS

Applying for Section 8 housing benefits begins by first locating your local housing authority office. Listings of state housing authority offices can be found at www.hud.gov/local/index.cfm. Once you have located your local housing authority, you will need to go to the housing authority office and complete an application for Section 8 housing, much as you did when obtaining Social Security benefits for your client. The more information you can bring to document the client's disability, the better. If the client receives SSI, SSDI, or Medicaid, be sure to bring the letter from the Social Security or local welfare/human services office indicating that the client's application for these benefits has been granted. This will help greatly speed up the process of applying for Section 8. Aside from bringing all the requisite information (e.g., Social Security card, letters from Social Security/Medicaid, pay stubs if available), the application process is not all that difficult, though it does require patience.

Once the application process is complete, the client will be placed on a waiting list—sometimes for quite a while—until another Section 8 voucher is available. During this time, there are two key tasks a case manager must accomplish. The first is helping the client find temporary housing until his or her voucher is granted. Usually, group homes, personal care homes, or other group living situations are available and affordable, even given the client's limited disability check (though not always ideal from the client's perspective). Connecting clients to these services as soon as possible is a must, since they will need a place to live until their vouchers come through. Asking other case managers and your mentor for help in accessing these services in your particular community is usually the best way to find out how to navigate them. Exploring the possibility of living with a family member is also an option, although since the client could be waiting more than a year for a Section 8 voucher, the family needs to know up front that taking the client in could be an extended arrangement.

Your second task while your client is waiting for his or her Section 8 voucher is to scout out the different housing options available when the voucher comes through. You can obtain from your local housing authority office information on the housing options for Section 8 vouchers in your area. Many of these offices have searchable databases online, accessible through portal.hud.gov/hudportal/HUD?src=/ states. Remember, if clients receive tenant-based vouchers, they can move anywhere that accepts a Section 8 voucher, but if they receive project-based vouchers, they will have to live in the so-called "projects." Major cities usually operate both types of voucher program, and project-based vouchers that could serve as temporary housing may be initially available until the more popular tenant-based vouchers become available. Regardless of the type of Section 8 program, do not wait until the voucher is available to begin looking for housing. The client needs to be ready to relocate to the new housing very soon after the voucher is granted. During this time it is also imperative that you keep in regular contact with the local HUD office. Monthly contact is usually sufficient, but if you change your contact information or the client receives a new case manager, the HUD office needs to know immediately. Being prepared with different housing options, staying in contact with the HUD office, and keeping contact information updated are crucial with this particular resource because if a voucher becomes available and the client cannot be contacted and claim it soon, he or she will be moved to the bottom of the waiting list and will have to start the wait for a voucher all over again. This usually means another year of waiting and does a horrible disservice to your client.

After the housing voucher is granted and an appropriate housing facility located, you will need to arrange for moving assistance and help prepare your client for moving into a new home. This can be a happy but stressful time for many individuals, so it is important to mobilize as many resources as possible to ensure a smooth and successful transition. Assistance with moving expenses can usually be obtained from your local housing authority. For clients transitioning to a more independent environment (e.g., from a group home to an independent apartment), we recommend that you keep in frequent contact (at least weekly) during the first months after their transition to ensure that everything is going well and the appropriate resources are in place to help them succeed. With your help, individuals will have found a comfortable and supportive place to call home and will have taken a major step toward a better quality of life. Stable housing will move them toward a more complete recovery from severe mental illness. They will have the foundation they need to turn their focus toward learning the social and work skills needed to become effective members of their communities.

❖ KEEPING IN TOUCH DURING THE PROCESS

If you think the process of applying for income, health care, and housing benefits is challenging for you as a case manager, just consider how difficult it must be for your clients. What is involved is their very survival! They do not know where they will live, whether they will have enough to eat, or how they will get the medication they are not even sure they want to take. During this period of linking clients to critical entitlements, clients are likely to be gravely concerned about the answers to these questions, especially since you cannot provide an immediate answer to them yourself. The process is usually long and better measured in months rather than weeks. A common trajectory is initial denial of benefits, followed by a lengthy appeal process. This is where you must remember that your job is to be not only a broker of resources but an arbiter of compassion, empathy, and hope. There is only so much paperwork you can complete and meetings you can have with the disability officer before you must let things take their course and wait for your next move. During this especially difficult time, you will find some strategies particularly useful for helping your clients cope:

- *Stay in touch.* Your work with your client will often come to a standstill while waiting to hear about Social Security or housing benefits. You will have placed bandages on the sore spots with temporary housing, medication samples, and enough charitable income to ensure your client doesn't starve. You have to remember during this period that while you are not filling out paperwork or brokering new resources, you still have a job to do. You have to stay in touch with your client and report on progress. The worst thing your client can imagine in this situation is not that she was denied benefits but that you might have dropped the ball on the case and she now has no one backing her up. You should stay in touch with your client at least monthly to reassure her that things are moving forward and you are still working hard to get her what she needs.

- *Provide hope.* While staying in touch with your clients and keeping them in the know about where things stand, your next job is to provide hope for your clients and be hopeful yourself. If clients ask you when benefits will come, you can provide hope even if you don't know, reassuring them that the process always takes time. Case managers often worry about providing false hope. In reality, they should be more worried about providing false pessimism. These benefits usually work out; the main question is how and when. In the meantime, you have to reassure clients, providing hope.

- *Provide realistic reassurance.* A part of providing hope involves providing reassurance that things will eventually come together for your clients. This reassurance needs to be realistic since you cannot guarantee that your clients will receive Social Security benefits or get the type of housing voucher they prefer. What you can do is reassure clients that there are many resources out there and that you are going to draw on your previous experiences to help people get through the wait for disability benefits. Providing this simple level of reassurance can make all the difference in easing your clients' minds while they are struggling to survive.

❖ COLLABORATING WITH COMMUNITY RESOURCE PROVIDERS

The coordinating of disability and housing benefits for your clients will represent a major undertaking on your behalf and will require substantial collaboration with other social service agencies, such as the Department of Public Welfare, Social Security Administration, and Department of Housing and Urban Development. While waiting to hear from these agencies, you will have to collaborate with other local service providers to obtain stopgaps in basic needs for your client. To be an effective collaborator and resource broker, you will need to adopt a clever work style that is assertive but friendly, positive, and, above all, collaborative. Client needs are often pressing, and so it is easy to become demanding of other community providers as you try to work in the clients' best interests. But other professionals have their own demands and priorities, so becoming impatient with them will only delay the process of getting your clients' needs met.

Perhaps the best approach to collaborating with other resource providers is one in which you offer to act as the key connection between what they can provide and the welfare of your client. When you discuss your role with community providers, you can emphasize both your need for their help and your willingness to help them with their task of getting resources to those most in need. To be effective in working with community providers, you should develop a range of providers with resources so you do not ask too much of any given program. There are always more clients than resources, and if you rely too heavily on one resource, you can develop a negative reputation that will indirectly have a negative impact on your client's access to services. For example, funds to support essential living costs while a client is waiting for benefits may be obtained from several sources: the county, local nonprofit organizations, or religious groups. Always relying on the county without accessing other possibilities in your community may result in the county unofficially prioritizing other clients.

Finally, it is important to remember that when you interact with other agencies to gain community resources to help your client, you are representing your whole agency. Your behaviors and your appearance matter. If you arrive for appointments in jeans and a T-shirt, you will not be seen as a credible professional. You should not regard those representing other agencies as adversaries but, rather, should be open to their ideas and suggestions, nonverbally sending the message that you are your client's advocate but also a professional who understands their rules and limitations and wants to cooperate in determining the best ways to meet client needs. Focusing only on attempting to get what your client needs without recognizing the difficulties encountered by those doing their own jobs is certain to rub other professionals the wrong way and decrease the chances that they will help. This is perhaps most important when working with such agencies as the Social Security Administration and Department of Public Welfare, where staff may be coping with a difficult work environment dominated by rules that can be inflexible. Taking the time to chat and form positive relationships will engage these professionals in helping you overcome the inevitable barriers in their process. For instance, it is no secret that the default decision for disability benefit applications leans toward the negative. You need to learn not only the rules and criteria they use to make their decisions but also how to communicate your client's essential needs effectively. An approach that is honest and sincere rather than demanding and adversarial will go a long way.

8

Managing Crises as a Case Manager

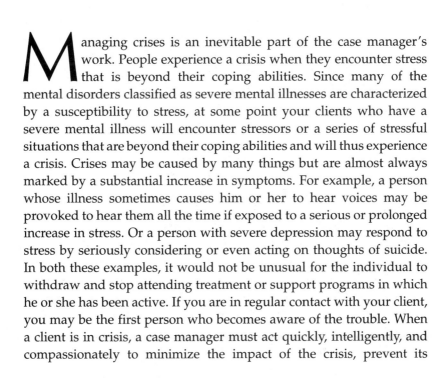

Managing crises is an inevitable part of the case manager's work. People experience a crisis when they encounter stress that is beyond their coping abilities. Since many of the mental disorders classified as severe mental illnesses are characterized by a susceptibility to stress, at some point your clients who have a severe mental illness will encounter stressors or a series of stressful situations that are beyond their coping abilities and will thus experience a crisis. Crises may be caused by many things but are almost always marked by a substantial increase in symptoms. For example, a person whose illness sometimes causes him or her to hear voices may be provoked to hear them all the time if exposed to a serious or prolonged increase in stress. Or a person with severe depression may respond to stress by seriously considering or even acting on thoughts of suicide. In both these examples, it would not be unusual for the individual to withdraw and stop attending treatment or support programs in which he or she has been active. If you are in regular contact with your client, you may be the first person who becomes aware of the trouble. When a client is in crisis, a case manager must act quickly, intelligently, and compassionately to minimize the impact of the crisis, prevent its escalation, help resolve the problem, and/or ensure the client's safety until the crisis is over. This chapter will provide an overview of the basics of how to manage some of the most common crises that occur for individuals seen in case management. You should know what to do when a crisis occurs and be able to act in a way that ensures the safety of everyone involved while at the same time respecting the dignity and preserving the autonomy of the individual as much as possible.

❖ PREVENTING CRISES

The single best method of managing crises is to prevent them from happening. Case managers often feel as though their job primarily consists of putting out fires, and, indeed, sometimes that is true. Your work can be characterized by having to manage frequent crises if measures are not taken ahead of time to prevent and prepare for them. It is possible to work with your clients to make a plan that involves stability and outlines steps to take when times become difficult. Such a plan will help your clients both experience fewer crisis events and know what to do to deal with stresses before they escalate. Avoiding unnecessary stress is always a good idea, because managing a crisis takes a toll on an individual's coping in general. It is possible to talk with your clients to learn what kinds of stresses are most difficult for them to manage. Most clients can tell you ahead of time what is likely to upset or provoke them and what has caused them trouble in the past. The best case managers talk with their clients ahead of time and come to know their clients' vulnerabilities and the situations they are likely to find most stressful. Identifying these issues or events allows both of you to keep an eye toward prevention and ensure the availability of appropriate resources to help the client.

Of course, life is stressful. Some stressful events are not predictable, and even positive events and things your client really wants, such as getting a job or going back to school, can be stressful. Since there is really no way to eliminate stress from life completely, in order to prevent a crisis that has the potential to be debilitating, a person must learn better ways to cope with inevitable stresses. *Some stress experienced by clients is internal or psychological,* such as that of experiencing persistent voices that tell them they are worthless or remembering past losses or traumatic events. For these types of stressors, psychological coping strategies will need to be developed through the use of medication, therapy, and ensuring the maintenance of a fairly structured, low-key environment.

While most individuals with severe mental illness who live in the community receive medication, many do not receive much psychotherapy that would help them learn effective coping skills. In fact, even the best case managers may not think to refer such individuals to therapy or are unable to find a therapist who would accept them. People with schizophrenia and other severe mental illnesses can benefit from psychotherapy, particularly the kind that will teach them strategies for avoiding and coping with psychological stress. A referral is certainly worth a try, especially if you note that a client experiences repeated stress-related crises. If you can find the client a therapist who will also work closely with you, you can play an important role in reinforcing the strategies your client learns by carrying them into the real world. In the long run, exposure to this sort of therapy could better equip these individuals to cope with life's stresses and dramatically reduce the number of crises they experience.

Although persons with severe mental illness may experience considerable psychological stress throughout their lives, your clients may also experience stress because of physical or material hardships. As we noted in the chapter on brokering resources, these types of stresses occur when they do not have the resources required to meet their basic needs (e.g., shelter, food). When basic and primary needs are not met, psychological stress is produced. The best way to manage these stresses is to be the best case manager you can be and use all your connections to help immediately get the client the resources he or she needs. As we have noted, it may take time to get housing or apply for food stamps, so temporary solutions are in order. Throughout these stressful times you will need to stay in especially close contact with your client and provide regular reassurance that more permanent solutions eventually will be obtained to make his or her life better. Physical stress does not need to last long before it can perpetuate a full-blown crisis, so responding quickly and efficiently is key. If you can mobilize resources quickly and provide gentle support, this will go a long way toward avoiding more serious trouble.

Stresses can also be produced by the client's *environment*. Living in or frequently encountering a social environment that is chaotic, overly critical, or disempowering will take a toll on a client's well-being. This could include living in a dangerous neighborhood in which the client is likely to be taken advantage of or teased, or when a negative psychological environment develops among a client's family, friends, or even treatment professionals. While there are some excellent methods of working with the family to reduce environmental stress, such as family psychoeducation,[1] many of these methods will be unavailable to the case manager and the community mental health system in which he or she works. Further, modifying stressful environments in other social settings is generally beyond the purview of the case manager. For individuals coming into repeated contact with these environments, perhaps the best thing the case manager can do is help clients find ways to exit situations that are becoming stressful. This may mean limiting contact with hypercritical friends and family, seeking more nurturing treatment providers, and increasing contact with more supportive companions, such as peer mentors. If frequent contact with these environmental stressors continues, the risk for psychiatric relapse is greatly increased. Consequently, helping consumers limit and avoid contact with environmental stressors as much as possible can be an excellent way to prevent future crises.

❖ DEVELOPING A CRISIS PLAN

There are many strategies you can use to help prevent a crisis from developing among your clients. However, no matter how good you are as a case manager or how many resources you can arrange, people will likely still experience a crisis or two at one point or another. While all crises cannot be prevented, a plan should always be in place to help minimize the impact of the crisis on the client and ensure that clients feel they are treated with respect and dignity during these vulnerable times. This plan is known as a *crisis plan*.

Crisis plans come in many different forms and can vary widely, but their essence remains the same. The goal behind a crisis plan is to specify ahead of time how a client would like to be treated if a crisis occurs. This includes specifying who the client would like involved in his or her treatment (e.g., doctor, case manager, family), what the treatment should be (e.g., medication, increased support, decreased environmental stimulation), and where the treatment should take place (e.g., a particular hospital, clinic, or community setting). Of course, some of these factors are nonnegotiable. If a client becomes dangerous to himself or others, a psychiatrist or medication will have to be involved. However, many other choices are optional and can be designed with respect for the client's preferences. Giving clients choices about their treatment, including specifying who is to be involved, can reinforce their autonomy and feelings of being respected

---

[1]See Anderson, Reiss, and Hogarty (1986).

and will help minimize the discomfort and demoralization associated with a crisis experience. If people can choose how a crisis is handled during the time they are well, they can have an increased sense of control later when a situation becomes seemingly uncontrollable.

Crisis plans are often developed within a larger *Wellness Recovery Action Plan,* or WRAP. This is usually a good idea, because as a recovery-oriented case manager, you want not only to help clients stay out of crisis but also to succeed in their lives. WRAPs move beyond a crisis plan by also specifying the optimal methods for daily maintenance that clients can use to keep themselves well and to move forward in their recovery. This will include formal treatment options such as medications and therapy but also less formal "treatments" such as keeping in contact with a close friend, setting aside time to relax and watch a favorite television show, or attending a supportive and friendly church. The goal here is to specify things clients are doing and should do when they are feeling well so the focus is not only on what is happening when they are at their worst. The major contents of WRAPs are listed in Table 8.1 and also include sections for identifying the early warning signs of getting sick and what helps the most when things are taking a turn for the worse. By developing these plans, you can not only help minimize the impact of a crisis but also help ensure that clients will remain well and achieve steady progress in their recovery.

❖ ASSESSING FOR THE RISK OF SUICIDE

Crises can be characterized by many different symptoms, but the most lethal and concerning symptom associated with a crisis is suicide. When individuals experience stress that seems inevitable and unrelenting, they may decide that a life full of stress is not worth living. When individuals have a severe mental illness, often with a long history of hardship, they are even more prone to entertain the possibility of suicide during a time of crisis. Consequently, it is vital for a case manager to know how to assess for suicide so steps can be taken to ensure the safety of individuals when they are not thinking clearly.

Suicide can be assessed by its four critical components: Specificity, Lethality, Access, and Proximity (see Table 8.2). These components can be easily remembered with the acronym SLAP. *Specificity* refers to how specific a person's plans for suicide are. There is less concern if a person has just been thinking of suicide than if she has in mind a specific method for killing herself, such as an available gun or bottle of pills, and a time when she knows she will be alone. *Lethality* refers to

Table 8.1   Elements of a Wellness Recovery Action Plan (WRAP)

1. Daily maintenance list

   a. What I am like when feeling well

   b. Things to do to stay well

2. Triggers

   a. Things that trigger symptoms

   b. What to do if triggers occur

3. Early warning signs

   a. What early signs look like

   b. What to do if early signs occur

   c. What I can keep doing (e.g., work) even with early signs

4. When things are breaking down

   a. What I look like when things are getting worse

   b. Things that can help reduce the breakdown

5. Crisis plan

   a. Symptoms that indicate others need to take over and the plan should be initiated

   b. Supporters (at least two)

   c. People not to be involved

   d. Medications to take and to be avoided

   e. Treatments and facilities

   f. Things that can help me stay in the community

   g. What I need others to do if I go to the hospital

   h. Deactivating the plan

Note: For more details on developing a WRAP plan, see Copeland (2002).

how deadly a person's plans for suicide are. Major concern should be afforded to those who plan to employ a highly deadly means for suicide, such as a gun or knife. Others may have plans for "parasuicidal" behavior, such as scraping their wrists with a nail file or burning themselves with a cigarette. These behaviors are serious but not as immediately lethal as plans involving a shotgun. *Access* refers to the suicidal person's ability to access the means to carry out the plan. A person who is planning to use a gun and has a gun in the house is at much greater risk than someone who has plans to use a gun but no immediate access to one. Finally, *proximity* refers to how close the person is to others who might reasonably help prevent a suicide attempt. Individuals who live by themselves and are generally isolated from others who care about their welfare may be able to commit suicide before anyone is able to intervene, whereas those living with a family member or in a therapeutic group home have at least the possibility of someone stopping them. In summary, when assessing for the risk of suicide, particular attention should be paid to individuals who have a clear and lethal plan achievable with little effort and who have no one around to stop them. Individuals without these high-risk characteristics should also be taken seriously, and as with any high-risk situation, you should never make lethality decisions on your own. Rather, you should travel in teams when doing crisis work, and your supervisor and mentor should always be informed of the situation. By following these assessment guidelines and spreading responsibility, you will protect your client and yourself.

Table 8.2   Elements of Suicide Assessment (SLAP)

Specificity—Is there a clear suicide plan? Is there a specific time, method, or location?
Lethality—How deadly are the planned methods? Are pills, guns, knives, or other weapons to be used?
Access—How realistic are the methods given what is available? Are deadly measures present in the house?
Proximity—Is there anyone around who could stop an attempt? Is the person living alone or with a caregiver?

❖ ACTING ON CRISES

When a crisis unfolds, a case manager can usually do one of three things. If the crisis is serious enough, you can get the client into the hospital. For less serious crises but situations severe enough that the client cannot be left alone, you can seek respite care. Finally, if there is no immediate or reasonable threat, you can proceed with close and careful monitoring and notification of the client's therapist and/or psychiatrist. Choosing among these options is difficult and should be a collaborative choice. You can use the suicide assessment above to help determine the seriousness of the crisis and the information below to determine how to apply your options during a crisis situation.

Hospitalization

If a client clearly represents an immediate harm to him- or herself or to others, the client will need to be hospitalized. Hospitalization is very difficult for both the client and the case manager, and involuntary hospitalization is particularly difficult. Nonetheless, a protected setting may provide the structure and support clients in danger need. Hospitalization procedures vary from state to state, but the best way to start the process is by calling the ambulance, as in any other medical emergency, and attempting to communicate with the client that you are going to get him or her help at the hospital. You should also notify your supervisor, mentor, and the psychiatrist if possible. Follow the ambulance to the hospital; once you arrive, you will need to provide the admissions staff with your information and the client's (e.g., medications, diagnosis, etc.).

There are likely to be times when a client who needs hospitalization does not want to go, requiring that you call the police instead of an ambulance. This is always a hard step for a case manager to take, especially when you know it is likely to have a negative impact on the trusting relationship you have taken such care to develop. It helps to remember that there really is no choice if the client's life is at stake. During this process, it is always important to remember to respect the client's dignity, explaining what you are doing and why. Being kind, caring, and sympathetic will go a long way toward maintaining your relationship and easing the client's mind during this very difficult process.

Once the client has been admitted, you will need to stay in contact with the hospital staff, such as the unit social worker, to keep up to date on how the client is doing and the plans for discharge. Hospitalizations usually do not last more than a week, so arrangements and discharge plans are often made quickly. If you can, visit the client and reassure him or her that you are there to support his or her recovery and well-being. Regardless, your client will not be in the hospital long, so you need to make sure you are prepared with whatever resources are necessary to help the client succeed when it is time to leave.

Respite Care

Respite care is an excellent alternative to hospitalization for those individuals who are less ill but still need supervision and frequent monitoring during a crisis. Respite care usually consists of a small-group living situation in a locked facility with a 24-hour nursing staff and daily visits from a psychiatrist. The environment is secured for safety but is small and not as overwhelming as a hospital setting. Individuals can usually leave for cigarette breaks but are required to stay on the respite center grounds. This arrangement can be particularly helpful for individuals who are clearly experiencing increased disorganization or psychotic thinking but are not dangerous to themselves or others. They just need to be someplace safe while they recover or while their medication is adjusted.

As when someone is hospitalized, entering a client into respite care requires the approval of a psychiatrist. So the first step in arranging respite care for a client is to call the local respite center and the client's psychiatrist to explain the situation. Sometimes the psychiatrist and the respite center will have to speak to each other before admitting the client; other times the respite center will admit the client provisionally and a psychiatrist will come and evaluate the crisis to ensure the client is receiving an appropriate level of care. As with hospital stays, the length of stay is usually not more than a week, so you will need to stay in daily contact with the respite team to be part of the discharge planning process and ensure that you can be available when the client is ready to leave.

Close Monitoring

Many times when clients are in crisis, they are not likely to harm themselves or others and their symptoms are not severe enough to warrant hospitalization or respite care. These crises are, nonetheless, serious and could evolve to the point where hospitalization or respite care becomes necessary. During such circumstances, all you can do is provide close and careful monitoring of the client to help prevent further deterioration and to spot such deterioration if it arises so a higher level of care can be sought. The case manager should visit individuals in such crises daily. They should also have the number of a crisis line ready so they can call if things get worse. While you usually will have created a general crisis plan, it is good to create a specific, time-limited plan for how to deal with this period. As always, your supervisor, mentor, and the psychiatrist should be notified when clients are in this state of emergency, as they are at an elevated risk for hospitalization and harmful behavior. If at all possible, it can also be helpful to obtain the assistance of a peer mentor who can visit the client for extended periods during critical times of the day (e.g., at night, when the client is especially lonely).

9

Identifying and Managing Substance Use Problems

S ubstance use is often a problem with mental and physical illnesses, and severe mental disorders are no exception. Current estimates indicate that as many as 50% of individuals with severe mental illness will also experience a significant substance use problem. Many individuals use substances to reduce symptoms that do not respond to medication or to escape a lifestyle that is unbearable without the euphoric effects of a drug. As a case manager, you need to be able to tell when a person you are serving has problems with substances, as it is very difficult (if not impossible) to treat mental health problems without also addressing the substance use problems that contribute to poor mental health. Just because you are a mental health case manager does not mean you can ignore substance use problems. Further, many legal and illegal substances can interact with psychiatric medications, reducing their effectiveness or increasing unwanted side effects, which will produce more problems than solutions for your clients. This chapter provides an overview of how to tell when a client you are serving has a substance use problem, what you can do about it, and strategies you can use to help such individuals help themselves.

❖ KNOWING WHEN SUBSTANCE USE IS A PROBLEM

Given that as many as 50% of individuals with severe mental illness experience problems with substances, you would be right a good proportion of the time if you just assumed everyone has this problem. This is the first important point of substance use assessment: Assume a substance use problem is a possibility with everyone. You will never know if you don't ask, and too many case managers believe they can leave this problem to other professionals. However, a case manager's job is to help get clients into the services they need, and substance use services (like many other services) are no exception. You are critical to the process of identifying substance use problems and finding services to address them. Consequently, *you should always ask every client you work with about their use of legal or illegal substances.*

The principles of substance assessment are simple and quite straightforward, although they can be difficult to implement consistently in practice. A good substance use assessment encompasses the following components:

- *Do not judge.* No one is going to admit to you that they are abusing illegal substances if you communicate an attitude that clearly condemns their problem. Our society often calls individuals who have substance use problems "junkies" or "winos," and there is an incredible stigma about admitting to such problems (doubly so if you have a mental illness). Whatever you ask during your assessment, be open and nonjudgmental. Your role is to help, not to judge.

- *Use multiple sources.* Family, friends, and other professionals can help provide important information that clients may be unable or unwilling to provide. If a substance use problem is suspected, information should be gathered from as many sources as possible to obtain a complete assessment of the level of substance use.

- *Suspect all substances.* Illegal drugs are but one type of substance individuals can become addicted to. Alcohol, prescription drugs, and even cough medicine can provide a buzz and are potentially addictive. Just because a client is not shooting heroin does not mean he is not habitually taking pain pills or drinking alcohol at levels that can influence his mental illness. Even legal drugs can be addictive and should therefore be considered in your assessment.

- *Assessment does not mean intervention.* When a substance use problem is uncovered, case managers tend to want to intervene right then and there. They will say, "You have to stop," or try to impose consequences on clients for their use. Trying to intervene with individuals who are not ready to change will stop the assessment process dead in its tracks. You are assessing to gather information in an impartial and nonjudgmental manner, not to intervene, threaten, or coerce. Gather the facts with an eye toward providing this information to the team in setting up treatment options and resources.

Now that you know a couple of the principles of a good substance use assessment, you might be wondering the practical ways you assess for substance use problems. Employing the basic principles, you can proceed to investigate substance use by asking targeted questions. Some helpful questions to include in any substance use assessment are listed in Table 9.1. These include asking about duration, frequency, context, and consequences of substance use. If you find that your client has been using substances often, for a long time, and while alone, and has trouble with the law, friends, work, or school, he or she likely has a significant substance use problem. The defining characteristic of substance abuse is that using substances has interfered with some important aspect of life in a significant way. Disruptions of friendships, troubled coworker relationships, and legal problems are areas of life that coincide with substance use problems, regardless of frequency or duration of use. Further, the use of illegal substances while alone is a good indication of a problem, regardless of whether there have been legal or functional repercussions. People with mental illness often already have significant relationship and functional challenges, but these are exacerbated significantly by the use of substances. For example, a client may begin stealing from family members to obtain alcohol or drugs. Other times, clients may become unusually withdrawn, more so than you have recognized in the past. Changes in these behaviors certainly warrant investigation of the potential for substance use problems.

❖ A CLIENT HAS A SUBSTANCE USE PROBLEM—NOW WHAT?

Chances are that 50% of your caseload will have some problem with substance use, so you will need to know right away how best to serve those who do. *The best approach for individuals with severe mental illness who also experience comorbid substance use problems is integrated treatment that addresses the mental health and substance use issues together.*

Table 9.1   Substance Use Assessment Questions

1. Have you ever tried (marijuana, cocaine, etc.)?
2. Do you ever drink alcohol?
3. Do you take any pain medication?
4. How often do you (drink, take painkillers, smoke crack, etc.)? How long have you been doing this?
5. Who do you do this with? With friends or sometimes alone?
6. When do you usually do this? On the weekends or during the week?
7. What do you do when you do this? Where do you do this?
8. How do you feel when you do this? Do you ever feel guilty?
9. What are the benefits of doing this? Are there any downsides? Have you ever had anything bad happen because of doing this?
10. What do other people think about you doing this?

Unfortunately, the mental health and substance abuse treatment systems are often deliberately kept separate, which means clients who have substance use problems will need to be enrolled in the separate substance abuse treatment system. Enrolling your clients in the substance abuse treatment system means calling an access number at a local substance abuse agency, making an appointment for assessment, and then setting up treatment options. Treatment options usually include some form of therapy, a drug monitoring program (through regular urine or blood testing), detoxification, and, for opiate addiction, drug replacement therapy (i.e., methadone treatment). Narcotics Anonymous and Alcoholics Anonymous are also excellent adjunct treatment options for individuals with substance use problems, and both can be relevant for alcohol and illegal drug users alike. Meeting information and contact numbers can be found on their websites (www.alcoholics-anonymous.org and www.na.org). Bottom line, the mental health system is not best equipped to serve individuals with substance use problems, and close collaboration with a treatment facility that specializes in substance abuse treatment is a must!

Although there are few options for the integrated treatment of mental health and substance use problems, some do exist, and you should be aware of them so you can refer clients to these resources when appropriate. The two most prevalent options include the dual disorders support groups *Double Trouble* and *Dual Recovery Anonymous*.

These support groups may be considerably more acceptable to your clients than Alcoholics or Narcotics Anonymous, as everyone in Double Trouble and Dual Recovery Anonymous will be experiencing both mental health and substance abuse problems, whereas this is not necessarily the case with the former support groups. In addition, a very small (but, we hope, growing) number of mental health facilities will have an *Integrated Dual Disorders Program,* which is an absolute necessity for any of your clients experiencing substance use problems. The benefit of this type of program is that there is a simultaneous and well-coordinated effort to treat both mental health and substance use problems, which are almost always interrelated and need to be treated as such. You will need to be careful not to overwhelm your clients with multiple treatment options for both mental health and substance use problems, which makes integrated programs more ideal. In addition, while you will likely be the first professional to notice substance use problems with your client, an addictions specialist should be involved immediately to obtain a thorough assessment and treatment recommendations.

❖ TIPS FOR WORKING WITH INDIVIDUALS WHO HAVE SUBSTANCE USE PROBLEMS

Individuals who have both a severe mental illness and a substance use problem can be difficult to serve, because they have so many needs and there are so few resources out there to help them. We have just identified some of the ways you can connect such individuals to treatment resources, which should help you get over some of the hurdles to providing the best care you can for these individuals. Of course, you would be kidding yourself if you thought that merely knowing and offering treatment options alone was going to work. Recovery from substance abuse is a process, and as most people know, this process begins with recognizing you have a problem. You are likely to be the first one to really investigate substance use problems with your clients, and, as such, the significant substance issues you uncover are likely to be in the early stages of recovery. This means many of these individuals will not even recognize they have a substance use problem and, therefore, will refuse most treatments offered. The best tip for working with individuals with comorbid mental health and substance use problems is to start with where they are in the process. The major stages of substance use recovery or "change" and their characteristics are listed in Table 9.2. As you can see from this table, treatment and abstinence from substances does not even begin until Stage 4 (the action stage). Consequently, the treatment options and resources you offer a client with comorbid substance use problems need to be sensitive to where they are in the stages of change.

Table 9.2   Stages of Substance Use Change

Stage	Characteristics
1. Pre-contemplation	Denial, lack of insight about the problem
2. Contemplation	Recognizes there might be a problem; conflicted about admitting to a problem
3. Preparation	Admits to a problem; ready to take some small steps toward treatment
4. Action	Fully commits to treatment and begins real behavior change
5. Maintenance	Abstaining from substances; trying to keep up treatment gains
6. Relapse	Has a temporary slip from abstinence; feels ashamed and guilty

Source: Prochaska and DiClemente (1983).

For example, individuals who are at the pre-contemplation stage need encouragement to take an objective look at their behavior and arrive at an honest assessment of the problems of their substance use. Individuals at the maintenance phase need encouragement to keep up their progress and support for staying connected with treatment resources. Most important, a relapse stage is built into the process, as repeated relapse is a part of a substance use disorder. Therefore, individuals who experience a relapse have not failed in treatment but, rather, have experienced an understandable temporary setback. What they need from you at this time, more than ever, is reassurance and support to get back on the horse and continue toward recovery. None of these processes is terribly linear, and the stages of change can run in a cyclical fashion. A person contemplating treatment can move back and forth from denial to contemplation for some time. The main goal for you when working with such individuals is always to target your approach to the stage the person is in. Providing something when the "time is not right" will result only in frustration on both your and the client's parts.

10

Comorbid Health Problems

The surgeon general estimates that individuals with severe mental illness will die 25 years younger than the rest of us. This is a tremendous amount of life lost, in many cases needlessly, just because of the presence of a mental health condition. Diabetes, obesity, and cardiovascular problems are at an all-time high among people with severe mental disorders. Some of these health problems have been brought on by the introduction of newer medicines with newer side effects. Others are due to a lifetime of poor self-care. Whatever the root cause, it is clear that many of the individuals you serve as a case manager will have significant health problems. From high blood pressure to chronic obstructive pulmonary disease, from hepatitis to HIV, and everything in between, individuals with severe mental illness often have significant physical health problems that can place their mental health in jeopardy and cannot be ignored. This chapter focuses on some of the most common serious physical health problems individuals with psychiatric disabilities experience. As the person who sees these individuals the most, you will need to look out for these issues and set up physician resources when you suspect problems. In the end, you may very likely save someone's life.

❖ HEALTH AND SEVERE MENTAL ILLNESS

Physical health care in the United States and other industrialized nations is improving every day. The state of medicine is constantly improving, treatments exist for diseases that were once fatal, and prevention is becoming more realistic for many of the ailments that were once lifelong problems. In spite of these advances in medicine, individuals with severe mental illness continue to receive very poor health care. Some of this can be attributed to the toll a mental illness takes on the physical body, which often results in poor health and neglect of physical health problems. There are, however, many other reasons for why individuals with severe mental illness receive poor health care, beyond their mental illness. Because such individuals often receive public medical assistance, which pays physicians at a very low rate, many doctors do not want to take individuals with mental illness into their care. In addition, most physicians have received little to no mental health training and often tend to dismiss the legitimate concerns of individuals with psychiatric disabilities as mere manifestations of their mental health problems. Individuals with schizophrenia and other severe mental illnesses are often already timid about confronting others in power and standing up for themselves, so many of their problems may go unnoticed even if they are routinely seeing a doctor. *In short, the primary care and medical system in the United States is not prepared properly to serve individuals with severe mental health problems.*

❖ YOU NEED TO ADVOCATE

Given that the physical health care system is so ill prepared to serve your clients, you will need to play an even greater role in ensuring that the people you serve receive the care they need and deserve. Often, this means you will need to go to the doctor with clients and advocate on their behalf. If people at the doctor's office are giving your client the runaround about scheduling an appointment (not unusual), you may need to accompany the client to the office to get things moving. If the doctor is not listening to your client's complaints, you may need to sit in on the appointment with him or her and reiterate that the problems are serious and legitimate. Most often, you can help by simply being a support for clients in an unhelpful or intimidating situation and encouraging them to share their problems openly and honestly with the doctor so they can receive adequate treatment. Some helpful strategies you can use to advocate on your clients' behalf to ensure they get the care they need are as follows:

- Prepare with your client ahead of time issues to be discussed with the doctor. Write these issues down if the client has trouble remembering.

- Bring a complete list of the medications your client is taking.

- Sit in on your client's appointment. Encourage your client to speak about his or her problems. Support your client's complaints by reiterating them to the doctor.

- Purchase a calendar and mark medical appointments in it.

As always, use a recovery orientation with this process, and never do more for clients than they need. You want to be a support and advocate, not someone who encourages complete dependence and negates the skills individuals have to accomplish many of these tasks on their own. For example, if clients are capable of preparing a list of issues themselves, encourage and support that. If clients can learn to remember all their medications, encourage them to learn this before they see the doctor. If you do it right, preparing for the doctor can be an excellent opportunity to teach skills and independence so the next time your clients need to see a doctor, they may be able to do it on their own.

❖ OBESITY AND DIABETES

Aside from needing to be an advocate to ensure that your clients receive the care they deserve, you will also need to be vigilant in the major health care issues that tend to plague individuals with severe mental illness today. Perhaps the two most serious and common physical health problems experienced by this population are obesity and diabetes. There are several reasons for this. First, newer medications (particularly second-generation antipsychotic medications) carry with them the very common side effect of weight gain. Some of these medications (see Zyprexa, or olanzapine) are even involved in class-action lawsuits because of the serious weight problems they can induce. Second, individuals with severe mental illness often do not follow a healthy diet (like many of us) and usually engage in little consistent physical exercise. This of course puts such individuals at an increased risk for physical health problems associated with weight gain. Finally, physical health care is terribly difficult to maintain with few resources and other major concerns in life (e.g., constantly hearing voices). As you might know, there are days when things are going badly and all you want to do is eat a pint of Ben & Jerry's, and on those days spending time exercising is especially hard. If you react this way to even minor psychological stressors, imagine how difficult it must be for someone with a severe mental illness to stay on a consistent diet and exercise plan. When you combine these three factors (medication side effects, poor diet/exercise, increased psychological distress), it is no surprise that many individuals with psychiatric problems struggle with weight issues.

Significant weight gain brings a whole host of serious physical health problems. Diabetes can develop, blood pressure can increase, bad cholesterol can increase, and good cholesterol can decrease. All these problems represent major risk factors for the No. 1 killer in the United States—heart disease. This undoubtedly accounts for the fact that individuals with severe mental illness die 25 years younger than those in the average population. Consequently, you will serve your clients well and possibly save their lives if you can spot the signs of obesity and diabetes and get them in to see the doctor as soon as possible. Major signs of weight problems and potential diabetes that should raise concern are listed in Table 10.1. As you can see, many of these signs can be easily detected by anyone who spends some time with the client. Of all the professionals, you probably spend the most time with the client and therefore are probably the best person to bring this information to the doctor's attention if you see a problem developing. Some simple tips for handling obesity and diabetes with your clients include the following:

- *Talk to the doctor.* Schedule an appointment with the doctor immediately if you see several signs of a weight problem.

- *Provide education.* Educating your clients about the seriousness of weight gain and diabetes is important. Many clients may not know how serious these problems can get, and while you do not want to scare them, you want them to be equipped to make informed decisions about their health.

- *Encourage better diet.* If you go out to eat with your client, go someplace healthy and model reasonable eating. If fast food is the only option, encourage the wasting of food (e.g., don't eat all the fries).

- *Help plan for more exercise.* Getting off the bus a couple of stops early can help. Getting your client involved in an exercise or walking program with others can keep up motivation.

- *Get that blood pressure checked.* Always have the nurse check your client's blood pressure when seeing the psychiatrist. Encourage the use of free blood pressure machines at the grocery store or pharmacy.

- *Discuss medication adjustments.* Bring weight issues to the attention of the psychiatrist and discuss possible alternative medications.

- *Involve a nutritionist.* Eating well is very difficult and requires substantial planning. Nutritionists can help plan healthy and enjoyable meals with your client so eating better becomes more routine and less difficult.

Table 10.1   Signs of a Weight Problem or Diabetes

1. Increased weight gain (10 pounds or more)
2. Increased belly fat, stomach size
3. Poor diet (lots of sugars and fat)
4. Frequent thirst
5. Frequent urination
6. Poor vision
7. High blood pressure
8. High cholesterol
9. Difficulty engaging in minimal exercise

❖ SMOKING AND TOBACCO

Another key health concern among clients with severe mental illness is their use of cigarettes and other forms of tobacco that have been clearly shown to have adverse health consequences. Individuals with severe mental illness, particularly those with schizophrenia, tend to smoke as though there is no tomorrow. There are many possible reasons for this. Smoking provides some low-level socialization, helps people deal with stress, and replaces other more harmful behaviors the client is trying to abstain from, such as using drugs or alcohol. Some research even suggests that nicotine serves to improve some of the symptoms of severe mental illness. Given all the positive functions smoking serves for your clients, why on earth would you want to help them quit? Well, because you want them to live a long, fun, and healthy life.

Smoking is a temporary solution for many of these problems, but on the way it is also extremely addictive. Too many clients die of lung cancer and emphysema and spend a good part of their better years carting around an oxygen tank. Smoking is not something you want to address immediately. Circumstances need to be stable, people need to feel secure, and you need to have a good game plan in place for how other things will serve the functions of smoking. When the time is right, there are a great number of resources you can call on to help your clients kick the habit, including the following:

- *Smoking cessation programs.* Almost all community mental health clinics worth their salt will have a smoking cessation program to help clients quit smoking.

- *Nicotine gum.* This is a good and much healthier replacement for inhaling nicotine, and one that is easier to give up.

- *Stress management techniques.* The skills discussed in Chapter 5 are helpful not only for managing the primary symptoms of mental illness but also for managing stress and helping individuals come to the point where they can manage their stress without smoking.

- *Prescription medications.* Several drugs on the market have shown benefits for helping individuals deal with a biological addiction to nicotine.

❖ BEYOND LIFE-THREATENING CONDITIONS

Obesity, diabetes, and smoking are some of the key factors that contribute to clients' losing so many years and dying at young ages. While addressing these areas is absolutely essential to help safeguard your client against serious health problems, they do not represent the vast array of other health considerations you will need to be mindful of when working with your clients. Many areas of clients' health get neglected when they are ill. While overlooking these areas may not kill your client, it can certainly make life difficult and miserable. Perhaps two of the most common of the non-life-threatening health problems you will need to keep an eye on are teeth and foot problems. For most clients, it will have been years since they have been to the dentist, and they may be in a considerable amount of pain due to infected gums and decaying teeth. Few will speak up about this, though, out of fear of going to the dentist. Just as too many clients die too young, too many clients are also in dentures too young. You would serve your clients well by helping them get and keep dental appointments.

In addition, foot problems tend to crop up more than you might expect with clients. Ingrown nails, poor circulation, broken toes, and other foot problems are not at all uncommon, yet it is easy to forget that clients are not likely to come to you with these issues. Some of these issues can grow into larger problems and even lead to amputation, while others are merely uncomfortable and can make walking and exercising difficult. You will need to work with your clients to get them podiatry appointments and check in with them about their feet. It should go without saying that all clients need to have at least a yearly physical workup, and the primary care clinician should check both teeth and feet. If not, be there to ask him or her about it, as these are some of the most common and uncomfortable health challenges your clients will face. These areas are but two examples to remind you that good health means addressing more than just life-threatening issues. The overall goal is for you to help your clients look out not only for serious health problems but also for those minor issues that can be a big pain.

❖ YOU'RE NOT THE DOC

All this probably seems like a lot of information, and more than you ever wanted to know about your clients' health problems—and, indeed, it is a lot to take in. If the physical health care system was doing its job and was well prepared to serve individuals with severe mental illness, you might not need to know all this. As it is, primary care physicians know little about the intricacies of mental health problems, and so you will need to help out by providing a bridge between the physical and mental health care systems. That said, it is important to remember that you are not the doctor and should never be in charge of making any major medical decisions. This is why you work in a team, with members of the medical profession being one component of that team. You should not feel responsible for meeting the physical health care needs of your clients; rather, you need to work with your team to relay pertinent information to the doctors who are in charge of keeping your client healthy. This means you need to know about health problems and resources to address health issues, but you are not responsible for treatment of these issues. Treatment is the doctor's job; linkage, support, and advocacy are yours.

11

Helping Clients Find Work and Stay Employed

The ultimate goal of recovery involves getting back into the mainstream of life, not just by developing relationships but also by contributing to society through competitive employment. Unfortunately, as many as 75% of individuals with severe mental disorders are not employed, even though nearly as many express a clear desire to work. Individuals with mental illness face many barriers to getting and sustaining employment. Some of the symptoms of their illness can be an impediment, especially their sensitivity to stimulation, social awkwardness, and lack of a recent work history. The stigma associated with mental illness also can contribute to their inability to get a job, and if their illness has been chronic, they are also likely to have lost the habits of consistent attendance and responsibility necessary to succeed in a work environment. Getting back into the workforce requires a gradual and supported process, including the support of disability benefits until clients have succeeded. The fact that clients will need to prove their disability continuously in order to receive benefits can undermine their confidence in this process. Despite these barriers, work is a real possibility for many individuals. This chapter will provide you with strategies you can use to help many of your clients achieve their dreams of going back to work.

❖ THE IMPORTANCE OF WORK

Before beginning to discuss some of the methods you can use to help your clients get back to work, it is worth underscoring the importance of work in the lives of individuals with severe mental illness. Research has repeatedly shown that when individuals can be integrated into society, they are happier, experience less severe symptoms, and are less likely to have a relapse that requires rehospitalization. Any sort of work helps these individuals reintegrate into society. Working facilitates a sense of connection with the world, a sense of making a real contribution by moving beyond the identity of "psychiatric patient." Work can also motivate individuals with mental illness to attend more carefully to maintaining their gains and interacting appropriately with others.

To facilitate the likelihood of the individuals you serve accomplishing these tasks, you can reinforce their visions of having a better life and connect them with the resources necessary for success. Rather than concentrating on their deficits and assuming they are too "fragile" to work, help them believe that the possibility of employment is an appropriate long-term goal. A focus on helping clients find work is not something many professionals do since it falls outside the usual focus of simply facilitating community survival. Rather than supporting only the interventions of medication, therapy, and other structured treatment regimes, we challenge you to consider helping the individuals on your caseload gradually move toward employment, even if they might seem currently unable to work.

❖ HOW TO SUPPORT EMPLOYMENT AS A CASE MANAGER

Timing is an important factor in moving your clients toward employment. Individuals just leaving the hospital after a psychiatric crisis are probably not the best candidates for immediate employment, since their first priority must be survival and stability. Once they feel relatively comfortable managing their illness outside of a protected setting, you can work with them to establish more ambitious goals and ways of achieving them. Stability is an important goal but not the only or final one. Rather than becoming content with the particular level of stability a client may have attained, look for signals and messages from clients that they are ready to try to move toward work, and be ready to respond to them. Don't become "gun shy" of the risks. Steps toward employment may be stressful, but taking these steps gradually with the proper supports in place will minimize the risk of relapse. A case manager can do many things to increase the chances of gaining employment for those they serve. The following are some basic tips you can use to get the ball rolling and keep it going once a client expresses a desire to work.

- *Assess and practice prework skills.* A focus on basic behaviors that will contribute to success in a work setting should come first. Check to see if your clients are used to getting up at a regular hour. If they are not, work on this task with them. Check to see if they are able to concentrate or are easily distracted. If they cannot focus, try tasks or games that build this ability.

- *Take one step at a time.* Employment is often best started gradually, perhaps through volunteering to develop further the work habits noted above. Depending on their level of skill and motivation, gradually help clients seek part-time, low-stress jobs that will build a work history that will help them eventually seek full-time employment. These low-level experiences allow clients to test the waters and gain confidence in their stamina and abilities before they move to more demanding work environments. Taking one step at a time will allow both you and your clients to determine their level of comfort and will prevent them from becoming overwhelmed with overly ambitious moves attempted too soon.

- *Make an appointment with an employment specialist.* Most, if not all, states run an Office of Vocational Rehabilitation, where people are tasked solely with the responsibility of helping disabled individuals get back to work. Getting an employment specialist from this office on your team can help clients who wish to work, as it will open the door to a number of important resources, such as vocational assessments, job placements, and even tuition reimbursement for additional training or higher education.

- *Make an appointment with a benefits counselor.* Work is within the rights of everyone, even those with disabilities. Getting a job can nonetheless cause problems with disability benefits and payments. The local vocational rehabilitation and/or Social Security office often has benefits counselors available to help determine how clients with disabilities can maintain living and health benefits as they move into the employment world. Contacting such individuals will help prevent your clients' disability payments from being prematurely discontinued when their work situation has not yet been stabilized.

- *Communicate the benefits of work consistently.* Individuals will experience periods of ambivalence about going back to work, partly due to fear of failure. To keep up their motivation, they need to hear supportive words from you and the rest of the team about the benefits of work and how you will support them in the process. If their fears become too great, an occasional step backward can allow a respite that will help them regroup and build confidence.

- *Ease fears of relapse.* Many individuals initially get sick in their teens and early 20s, just when they are starting out in their lives. This means they may have little or no work history. In addition, they may equate the stress of a job with their initial breakdown and may fear that getting a job will cause them to unravel again. Fears such as these further stress the importance of small steps toward employment that promote the experience of small successes that build confidence. As you work with your clients to accomplish such tasks, you can provide hope and help, reassuring them that supports will be in place and you will be there for them.

❖ TIPS FOR GETTING PAST THE BARRIERS TO EMPLOYMENT

As you can see, there are a number of concrete things you can do to help facilitate your client's goal of getting back to work. Many of these tips will go a long way in helping set the stage for successful employment. However, barriers are often still present. Individuals may not have the skills they need to start working, vocational counselors may be unavailable, and Social Security may start discontinuing disability benefits. All these things can be common and significant barriers to maintaining employment. While employment specialists can help your client overcome these barriers, it is often up to you to make suggestions for strategies to support work and deal with its repercussions. Below are some guidelines and concrete suggestions you can implement when the barriers to employment pop up or, even better, options you can put in place when you suspect certain barriers will be a problem.

Supported Employment

Many individuals with severe mental illness will need more than a job opportunity and support from you to succeed at work. Often, individuals have been unemployed for a lengthy period, may have lost many skills, and may be unprepared for the work environment. This is where supported employment programs can really make a difference. Supported employment is a type of job training and support program where individuals are placed at a "real" competitive job that matches their preferences and abilities. At the job, a coach works alongside clients for a finite time to teach them the necessary work skills and behaviors to maintain the job. The job coach gradually decreases the time he or she spends with clients as they gain proficiency, with the eventual goal of clients maintaining their work status independently. This is one of the most effective ways of ensuring job success for individuals who have been out of work for an extended period, as supported employment provides tangible, close, hands-on guidance at work.

Another variation of supported employment is the clubhouse model. The clubhouse is a community partnership between professional staff and clients with severe mental illness that offers a place for clients to be part of a community and participate in recreational activities. In this regard, the clubhouse serves an important function of facilitating socialization. A unique feature of the clubhouse, beyond this social rehabilitation, is that it is run by both staff and clients. The key therapeutic focus of a clubhouse program thus moves beyond socialization to job training. Clients who work at the clubhouse learn how to manage a work day and perform the functions needed by the clubhouse to support its members, such as organizing and developing activities, cooking, cleaning, and managing funds. The clubhouse becomes an actual job site that allows many to learn work skills in a supportive and understanding environment. Many mental health and vocational rehabilitation agencies are now implementing supported employment and clubhouses as evidence-based practices, so while there is no central resource for available programs, your mentor, supervisor, or one of your fellow case managers likely knows about such a program in your area. For the many clients you serve who want to work but are unable to do so because of a lack of experience or job training, supported employment can be a way to overcome this critical work barrier.

Ticket to Work

The benefit-friendly Ticket to Work program is another program that can be quite useful for clients who are vocationally ready to work but who are receiving disability health insurance benefits that might be jeopardized by increased earnings. This program was designed to provide additional services (such as supported employment) to individuals with disabilities who want to go back to work. In part, the program is meant to remove work disincentives inherent in the disability benefits and Social Security laws, which actually discourage work by revoking key benefits (particularly health insurance) once employment begins. With the Ticket to Work program, individuals can work and earn money (below the state maximum threshold) for a limited time without losing Medicaid and/or Medicare benefits.

Enrolling in the Ticket to Work program is easier than enrolling in some others because it is supported by the federal government. To get a "ticket," your client can call the national toll-free number for enrollees (1-866-968-7842, or 1-866-833-2967 for the hearing impaired). The details of the program are somewhat lengthy, but a program specialist will provide a review for you and your client. The three things you need to keep in mind when enrolling are (1) tickets are time limited (usually about 9 months), (2) the more money your client makes the less he or she will receive from Social Security, and (3) medical coverage will continue by the Social Security Administration's suspension of medical review for your client as long as the ticket is being used. The program is seen as transitional, which is why it is time limited, and as such may be the most beneficial for individuals who could realistically get back to full-time employment and completely support themselves with their income. You should always try to talk with a benefits specialist before beginning the enrollment process, as a number of rules and regulations govern who can participate in the program and how increased income will affect your client's disability benefits. More information on the Ticket to Work program and other Social Security disability benefits information can be found in the Social Security Administration's Red Book, available online at www.socialsecurity.gov/redbook.

Dealing With Medicaid and Social Security

While the Ticket to Work program can help ensure medical benefits continue once work starts, it does not protect clients from losing money from Social Security as work-related earnings increase or from becoming ineligible for Medicaid and Social Security programs if earnings are too high. Below is some information about dealing with the often problematic intersection between increasing work and decreasing disability benefits.

- Social Security and Medicaid offices always need to be notified immediately if your client begins or stops working.

- Clients can earn a maximum of $1,000 a month outside the Ticket to Work program and still remain eligible for some benefits.

- Supplement Security Income/Social Security Disability Insurance payments will be reduced for up to half of everything your client earns on the job after the first $85 (i.e., Supplemental Security Income check reduction = [earnings − 85]/2).

- Clients can have a maximum of $2,000 in total assets (i.e., savings, checking, etc.) and still remain eligible for disability benefits.

As always, it is not recommended that you try to figure all this out on your own. The rules change frequently, and a benefits counselor is always an important person to contact when work is on the horizon. In addition, your supervisor, mentor, and/or colleagues will also be helpful informants for both you and your client as you learn the complicated ropes of the work and disability game. By taking these factors into account and putting into place the proper supports, your client should be able to begin working and succeed on the job without worrying about losing the financial or health benefits necessary for survival.

12

Taking Care of Yourself

The strategies outlined in this book were designed to help you become an effective case manager. Its collaborative strength-based approach should not only make your work more successful and rewarding but also help you maintain a level of morale that will give you the energy to care, listen, connect, and think creatively about how to help your clients. But while case management is gratifying, it is also challenging. The work is often hard, the hours long, and the pay relatively low. There will always be difficulties and pressures that influence the fabric of your professional life. In busy times, even your supervisors and mentors may have little time to provide you with encouragement and immediate rewards for doing the right thing. It isn't that they don't care or don't appreciate what you do; they are just busy keeping everyone on the mother ship afloat.

Under these circumstances, even if you are the best and most independent case manager, it is easy to become exhausted and demoralized about the clients you see, feeling that no one else really cares about the clinical challenges you encounter or the quality of the case management you provide. However, there are ways you can prevent or delay the development of compassion fatigue or even burnout. Whatever the difficulties of your working environment, you can find ways to nurture your professional soul—ways to take pride in the fact that your work is meaningful, honorable, and worthy of respect. However, maintaining good morale over time doesn't just happen; you have to work at defining your job and taking care of yourself.

❖ WHAT EXACTLY IS BURNOUT?

Experiencing job stress at various points in your case management career is natural and inevitable. As you spend days, months, and years attending to the mission of helping, you may become immersed in habits and neglect your own needs in ways that make you less effective with your clients and less satisfied with your job. You may even come to feel guilty about having needs, much less wanting your turn to have them addressed.

Table 12.1 lists some common signs of burnout. Burnout has been classically conceptualized as three interrelated domains: exhaustion, cynicism, and inefficacy (Maslach et al., 2001). Together, they make a particularly challenging mixture that can rob you of your best skills as a case manager and undermine your effectiveness with your clients. However talented you are, your energy will ebb and flow over the course of time, and you will experience periods when you are running

Table 12.1   Example Signs of Burnout

1. Exhaustion
2. Constantly feeling drained
3. Having enormous difficulty getting going in the morning
4. Having little to no energy after work or during the weekend
5. Cynicism
6. Feeling negative about and detached from your clients and colleagues
7. Wanting to leave work as soon as you get there
8. Difficulty seeing anything related to work as positive
9. Inefficacy
10. Frequently feeling incompetent
11. Feeling as though you never get enough done at work
12. Questioning whether this is the right job for you

on empty—times when you find it difficult to reach out to your clients and attend to their needs. The most experienced and committed case managers—even those who usually think of their jobs as exciting and rewarding—will sometimes become disenchanted and wonder why they chose this line of work. The clients you see may even sense your distance and react in ways that will leave you even more drained. The key to minimizing the impact of these times is to prevent a few bad days from degenerating into burnout or to remediate early symptoms of burnout before they can take hold. If you don't do something about these feelings, over time the life will go out of your work and you will find yourself in a daily struggle with your job as a case manager.

❖ WHY TAKING CARE OF YOURSELF IS IMPORTANT

There are things you can do in advance to protect yourself from exhaustion, and ways to handle job stress that will allow you to maintain the energy to care for your clients and yourself. Remember, there is a good reason airplane personnel instruct you to put on your own oxygen mask first. They know that only by taking care of yourself can you effectively help others. This chapter is meant to remind you that you can be a good case manager by defining your job in ways that do not always put your needs on the back burner. It would be nice if there was one right way, but there isn't. Each case manager needs to find his or her own unique way to stay alive and well, but there are some basic methods to prevent burnout and some basic strategies to help manage it when it occurs. The ideas below are not the proverbial rocket science but, rather, hard-won knowledge and suggestions to start you thinking about how basic practice skills and self-maintenance strategies can help you.

❖ GUIDELINES FOR THE ONGOING NURTURANCE OF YOUR PROFESSIONAL ENERGY AND SPIRIT

Remember Your Mission

You have chosen a career whose mission involves facilitating the survival of individuals with mental illness and helping them return to productive life in the community. This puts you, as a case manager, in the important position of providing the very foundation of community treatment. You will see all types of clients and will be responsible for meeting many of their basic physical, social, and personal needs. You will help them by providing hope for a better future and support that will allow them to accomplish both mundane and ambitious tasks. No one ever said being a case manager would be an easy job. You will help clients achieve their goals and provide a context in which they can survive and grow.

It is easy to forget how important your mission is to client survival when your daily focus is on tasks that sometimes seem small and endless, but staying aware of your overall mission is one of the most important ways you can both help your clients and maintain your own morale. If you keep an eye on the prize of the long-term goals, the importance of the daily small tasks becomes clear. To paraphrase a statement one of our colleagues made, you cannot change the cards your clients were dealt, but you can help them learn to play a poor hand well.

Define Your Job in Ways That Make It Doable

Being a professional means doing whatever it takes to get the job done. You will sometimes work long days, put in excessive hours, and go several extra miles to provide what your clients need. But those other days, when the demands on your time and energy are minimal, you can take time for yourself. Chances are you are not Superman or Wonder Woman, so you should take advantage of these times when you can take it easy.

Your ability to control your schedule so you can have protected time will be enhanced by discussing with your clients the limits of what you can do. Of course you have to handle any emergencies when they occur, but you don't have to let everything be an emergency. As part of developing a contract with your clients about the work you will do together, teach them the kinds of things they should regard as emergencies and what they should not. Let them know that you will attempt to be immediately available when these criteria are met and will get back to them in a reasonable time for all other concerns. Then assess how appropriately they use their access to you, and respond accordingly. Obviously, the risk of someone getting hurt or sent to jail is an emergency, but deciding what to buy for dinner is not. Most clients will not misuse your time, although those with personality disorders may. If you provide consistent feedback on the rules, your clients will respect them and you as a case manager.

The early discussions you have with your clients should also involve helping them choose realistic and attainable goals that will not frustrate them or you. Not everything can or should be fixed, and often what it would take to fix a minor issue is not worth the price. If you accept the fact that there are few long-term answers, and that even temporary ones work only temporarily, you and your client can avoid stress. Creating realistic goals and agreed-on responses to troublesome events will decrease your tendencies to become frustrated and depleted.

Nurture Yourself

Keeping up your morale involves accepting that your needs are legitimate and deserve your attention. No one else is going to be as invested in your well-being as you are. Only you can put your needs first, at least some of the time. Self-care begins by paying attention to your physical and mental health by getting enough sleep, eating right, and exercising when you can. Listen to your body and use stress-management strategies when you get aches and pains or migraines. Emotionally, as best you can, maintain an attitude of self-acceptance, avoiding negative self-talk that depletes your energy. In work and at home, focus on the positives, not on mistakes and what has gone wrong. In other words, carry your strength-based practice principles into your own life. If it's good for your clients, it's good for you. We all make a ton of mistakes over the course of our careers, regardless of the amount of training and life experience we accumulate. Be tolerant of your own mistakes, learn to let things go, and forgive yourself.

At work, take full advantage of those specific days when you have opportunities for respite. Take an extra few hours to have lunch or read. Even when the day is busy, take a few minutes to stretch, walk, or, if you are on the road, stop for coffee or to meditate. On a larger scale, keep yourself whole by maintaining a healthy balance between your professional and personal lives. We all have different levels of needs and interests at different points in time. Some of us thrive on work, and some of us do not. There will be times when your personal life must take precedence and times when the demands of the job must come first. There are times when either will be more satisfying to you than the other. The overall principle for morale maintenance is not to make your work your life, letting it seep into all your other priorities.

If you have difficulty setting reasonable limits on your work, try to find a personal passion or make time for play. We cannot say how, since what nurtures some would be a burden for others, so choose pursuits that suit you and decrease your stress. The idea is to avoid being too civilized to enjoy yourself with people and activities that are gratifying. If socializing gratifies you, socialize. If you prefer time alone, take up gardening or make time for solitary reading or piano lessons. Get involved in religion if you have one, or sports if you play one. Personal passions are not just an excuse to avoid our duties and obligations. Certainly, responsibility, duty, meeting obligations, and staying the course are important, but it's okay to not always defer your needs to the requirements of your job, your partner, or even your children. You will end up running on empty if you never get a turn. It is not a favor to your clients or your family/friends to let yourself become drained. Nurturing yourself is like building a fence at the top of a dangerous cliff to avoid having to put an ambulance at the bottom.

Develop Mutually Supportive Relationships With Colleagues

In case management, everyone is busy, often on the road alone with clients or finding ways to connect them with resources. The work can be difficult and isolating. If you are really lucky, your agency will have provided you with supervisors and mentors who view attending to your morale as a legitimate focus. They should, because there is plenty of evidence that good worker morale impacts both client outcome and staff turnover. However, some agencies are unaware of the importance of staff morale or don't know what to do to maintain it. Living with disagreement of organizational priorities can be a major source of burnout. If you work in a large organization and are far removed from the decision making that influences your work, you easily can come to feel like just a cog in the machine, and a sense of helplessness may set in.

You do not need to accept this state. If your particular work setting doesn't automatically take responsibility for attending to the morale of its workers, you can and should take the initiative to create an oasis of mutual support with other case managers. Everyone needs support, not just clients. Rather than competing with one another, you can create a work climate of nurturance, mutual support, and respect. Have meetings or brown bag lunches to share your experiences, but don't allow them to degenerate into gripe sessions or competitions about who is working hardest, who is the most skilled, or who has the most difficult clients. If you can, establish norms that emphasize helping one another. This will give you a cognitive life raft to temper the hard work of case management with mutual support and appreciation. Supporting your colleagues is like putting money in a bank—one you can count on being there for you, too, when you need to withdraw some support.

Remain Open to New Learning

Even once you have established solid skills and implemented effective interventions, it is always good to find ways to do things differently. There is no one right way to help clients who live with mental illness, no one size that fits all. Putting yourself on automatic pilot tends to get stale and boring over time. Boredom is not good for morale, and case management dominated by habit becomes less human. Every so often, shake yourself loose from whatever entrenched position you hold. Rather than trying to fit client issues into your view of reality, admit there are things you don't know and let your clients teach you. Admitting ignorance can be good for you and can open you up to new possibilities for learning how to help people.

❖ WHEN BURNOUT OCCURS

Even when you follow all the guidelines we have listed for preventing burnout, sometimes stresses can begin to influence your morale before they even register on your radar. When you are busy, it is easy to start just managing your life rather than living it, to tolerate your relationships with clients rather than taking some pleasure in helping them. Sometimes the strain is directly related to your work or clients (i.e., clients who are angry, whose behaviors push your buttons, or who are entrenched in negativity). If your caseload has too many of these clients, or does not also have clients who provide you with the satisfaction of feeling you are helping them, your work life gets hard. Even friendly clients can drain your emotional resources and cause compassion fatigue. Lots of things drag case managers into burnout, but remember that the most likely symptom is a gradual loss of a sense of mission. You have to have a goal you can believe in.

There are, however, a range of other reasons for a sudden loss of morale, so it is good occasionally to take stock of the stresses and problems you are experiencing to put yourself in a better position to address the causes of your stress and get back on track. We could list some possible sources of stress, but what is stressful to some will not be to others. For instance, some workers are depleted by long hours, while others thrive on them. Some case managers will find resistant clients challenging, but others will find them only frustrating. Review systems to examine the balance between your work and personal life, the climate of your work group, your sources of gratification and pleasure, the amount of support you get from superiors and colleagues, and whether you are in touch with new experiences. Look also at the long-term coping mechanisms you are using, particularly those that allow you to only tolerate a problem rather than solve it. Distractions and denial will work for only so long. In these times when your morale needs a boost, consider taking new risks, nurturing a passion (or several mini passions), and readjusting your work/pleasure ratio.

❖ SUMMARY

If you have read this manual cover to cover, you now know a little more about what will be expected of you as a case manager. You have an idea of what you are likely to experience with your clients and some of the key ways you can help them get the resources they need to manage their illness and their lives. The strategies emphasized throughout this book should make your work less stressful and, consequently, less draining. Maintaining a collaborative, strength-based focus with your clients will sensitize you to their needs, goals, and priorities and contribute to your morale by saving you the exhausting struggle of imposing your ideas on people who do not want to hear them. This focus prevents you from pushing your clients into changes they don't want to make and decreases energy wasted in dealing with unnecessary resistance. These general guidelines should prevent some of the exhaustion that can contribute to low morale.

This final chapter should have further reminded you that you became a case manager and got into the mental health business because you are committed to helping others. If you wanted big money, glory, and fame, you probably wouldn't have chosen this field. So if you feel envious of peers experiencing the financial benefits of moving up a corporate ladder, remember that *your* dreams involve the admirable goal of helping people in need. You may not make millions, but the rewards are many and total self-sacrifice is not required. Good case management is intertwined with good self-care, and your humanity is what provides the glue in your relationships with clients. Your ability to continue helping anyone depends on how well you take care of yourself.

References

Anderson, C. M., Reiss, D. J., & Hogarty, G. E. (1986). *Schizophrenia and the family: A practitioner's guide to psychoeducation and management.* New York: Guilford.

Copeland, M. (2002). *Wellness Recovery Action Plan.* Dummerston, VT: Peach Press.

Hogarty, G. E. (2002). *Personal therapy for schizophrenia and related disorders: A guide to individualized treatment.* New York: Guilford.

Maslach, C., Schaufeli, W. B., & Leiter, M. P. (2001). Job burnout. *Annual Review of Psychology, 52*(1), 397–422.

National Association of Case Management. (2005). *Personal practice guidelines.* Lincoln, NE: Author.

Prochaska, J. O., & DiClemente, C. C. (1983). Stages and processes of self-change of smoking: Toward an integrative model of change. *Journal of Consulting and Clinical Psychology, 51*(3), 390–395.

Social Security Administration. (2011). *Disability benefits.* Washington, DC: Author. Retrieved February 1, 2012, from http://www.ssa.gov/pubs/10029.html

Substance Abuse and Mental Health Services Administration. (2004). *National consensus statement on mental health recovery.* Washington, DC: Author.

Index

About the Authors

Shaun M. Eack, PhD, is Assistant Professor of Social Work at the University of Pittsburgh. His work focuses on the development of novel psychosocial interventions to facilitate the recovery of individuals with severe mental illness, as well as methods to support and enhance the community behavioral health workforce. He has published numerous articles on the treatment of individuals with psychiatric disabilities and has served as a practicing case manager and social worker.

Carol M. Anderson, PhD, is Professor Emerita of Psychiatry at the University of Pittsburgh School of Medicine. She has dedicated her career to helping individuals and families experiencing mental illness. Her recent work has concentrated on developing strategies of engagement and improving access to quality care for low-income and disenfranchised individuals.

Catherine G. Greeno, PhD, is Associate Professor of Social Work at the University of Pittsburgh. Her work is directed toward bridging the rigor/relevance gap between academic research and community mental health practice. She has held local, state, and federal grants supporting this work and is the author of numerous articles addressing various aspects of practice.

c

⊛SAGE research**methods**

The essential online tool for researchers from the
world's leading methods publisher

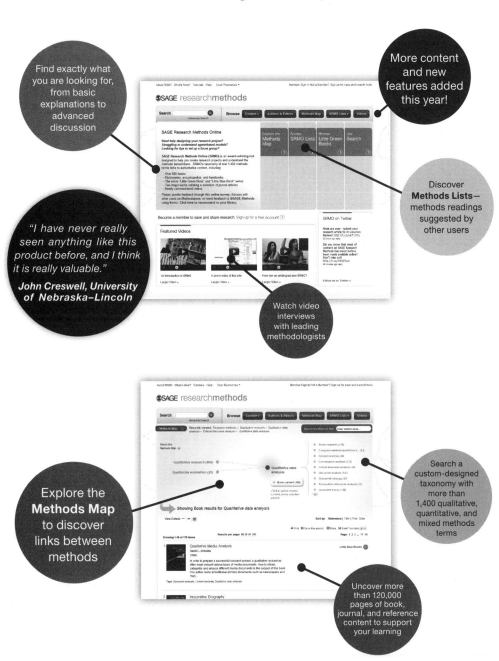

Find exactly what
you are looking for,
from basic
explanations to
advanced
discussion

More content
and new
features added
this year!

Discover
Methods Lists—
methods readings
suggested by
other users

"*I have never really
seen anything like this
product before, and I think
it is really valuable.*"
**John Creswell, University
of Nebraska–Lincoln**

Watch video
interviews
with leading
methodologists

Explore the
Methods Map
to discover
links between
methods

Search a
custom-designed
taxonomy with
more than
1,400 qualitative,
quantitative, and
mixed methods
terms

Uncover more
than 120,000
pages of book,
journal, and reference
content to support
your learning

Find out more at
www.sageresearchmethods.com